FORGOTTEN PIECES

Five Necessary Keys to Knowing and Following Jesus

JAMIE JOHNSON & MOLLY JOHNSON
A Boy With a Ball Resource

Forgotten Pieces
by Jamie Johnson and Molly Johnson
Copyright © 2023 Jamie Johnson and Molly Johnson

ISBN 978-1-63360-229-8

Scripture quotations are taken from THE HOLY BIBLE: New International Version ©1978 by the New York International Bible Society, used by permission of Zondervan Bible Publishers. All rights reserved.

For Worldwide Distribution
Printed in the U.S.A.

Urban Press
P.O. Box 8881
Pittsburgh, PA 15221-0881
412.646.2780

*Dedicated to Every Young Person Across the World—
those we know, love, and fight for, and those we do
not know yet*

Acknowledgments

There are many who gave themselves to the discovering, understanding, and living out of these five **Forgotten Pieces**. We acknowledge them with gratitude and deep love.

First, we acknowledge our original Boy With a Ball Team who paid a price to discover and live out the **Forgotten Pieces**:

> Emiliano Alvarado, Sam Chen, Anna Currie, Beth and Thomas Hernandez, Jody Lundy, John and Candace McCarter, Chris and Kelli Mora, Ryan and Magen Quiroz, Matt and Lauren Sartor, Melissa Tankersley, Peter and Melissa Watts, and James Williams

Next, we acknowledge the leaders who taught us to hear and obey God's voice, who wrestled these things out, and who cared for us in the journey:

> Dennis and Carol Anne Braswell, Keith and Patricia Currie, Leroy and Judy Curtis, Kevin and Dudley Davenport, John and Ellen Duke and the entire family at Covenant Life Church in Lawrenceville, GA, Brian and Kathy Emmet, Dr. Robert and Sue Grant, Gary and Sharrol Henley, Chris and Donna Hyatt, John and Judy Lowry, Jim and Debbie Matthias, Jim and Diane Newsom, Randy and Linda Reinhardt, Charles Simpson, Grant and Stacy Simpson, Stephen Simpson, John and Kathy Stanko, David and Marilyn Thompson, Mark and Caren Woodruff, and Hugo and Alice Zelaya and the entire family at Nueva Esperanza Church in San Jose, Costa Rica

To the authors and examples in faith whose works inspired us to grow deeper in knowing Him:

> Jackie Pullinger and the team at St. Stephens Society, Dr. Robert Coleman, and Brother Lawrence.

We recognize Cindy Chen and Christine Torres Emmet who played a critical role in the creation of this book.

Finally, we acknowledge the *Boy With a Ball* local teams and the young people they work with in San Antonio, Texas, San Jose, Costa Rica, Managua, Nicaragua, Atlanta, Georgia, Enugu, Nigeria, Nairobi, Kenya, Boston, Massachusetts, Addis Ababa, Ethiopia, and Beirut, Lebanon for giving their lives to live out the Forgotten Pieces and help others reach their God-given dreams.

Contents

Preface

On the last day of February in 1964 at Second Baptist Church in Detroit, Michigan, Martin Luther King Jr. preached a sermon from Luke 2:41-52.

The passage tells the story of Joseph and Mary going up with 12-year-old Jesus to the Feast of Passover in Jerusalem. According to the law in Jesus' day, every male was required to go to Jerusalem for the three great festivals each year (Deuteronomy 16:16). The Passover was the most important of these festivals and was followed immediately by the week-long Feast of Unleavened Bread. Joseph, Mary, and Jesus traveled to and from the feasts in a caravan for protection from robbers along the Palestine roads.

After the feast ended, Joseph and Mary's group traveled an entire day back to their hometown. They, in Dr. King's words, "stopped, I imagine to check up, to see if everything was all right, and they discovered that something mighty precious was missing. They discovered that Jesus wasn't with them. Jesus wasn't in the midst." Both husband and wife thought they had Jesus, only to find out, a day's journey down the road, that they had left him behind. "When they did not find him," Luke says, "they went back to Jerusalem to look for him" (Luke 2:45).

"Now, the real thing that is to be seen here is this:" King preached, "that the parents of Jesus realized that they had left and that they had lost a mighty precious value. They had sense enough to know that before they could go forward to Nazareth, they had to go backward to Jerusalem to rediscover this value. They knew that. They knew that they couldn't go home to Nazareth until they went back to Jerusalem. Sometimes, you know, it's necessary to go backward in order to go forward. That's an analogy of life."[1]

This book exists because we, like Joseph and Mary, have left some mighty precious pieces behind in our pursuit of Jesus and His ways. There are some critical tools, some **forgotten pieces,** that are taught and used throughout the entirety of the Bible. They are essential to Jesus' ministry, but unfortunately, aren't present or functioning in the lives of many who say they follow Him today.

This book is an equipping tool. It's not the kind of book you read once and forget about or place on some bookshelf. This is the kind of book you keep in your backpack, in the backseat of your car, on your e-reader, or even in your back pocket. It will be a resource and a help for you to get to what you're after.

This book contains five important but **forgotten pieces** that will take time and practice to get the hang of. They're supernatural, and they're also practical. They're not things you simply memorize. They're things that require action.

Two thousand years ago, Jesus walked into a religious world and confronted people with the ugly parts of religion so boldly that the religious influencers of the time had no choice but to kill Him. Jesus lived a life that, sadly, had little in common with churches today. He lived vividly, motivated by a love that would change the world— a love never seen before. He came into a hurting world and invited a small group of young people to follow Him to help people overcome the things that were ruining and suffocating them.

His life was inspirational, intriguing, and filled with compassion. His actions were powerful, creative, and life-changing. His words were compelling and mysterious at times, yet consistently warm and inviting. The Jesus you find in the Bible and across the pages of this book may surprise you and change your life—just as He did those who encountered Him back then.

This book is the product of a two-decade long journey that has taken us all across the world. Our organization, Boy With a Ball, was founded in 2001 to reach young people and help them know and follow Jesus. Boy With a Ball is an international non-profit entity with member organizations and ministry teams in cities across the world. The **Forgotten Pieces** are five things that we have found are essential but often missing for young people and leaders who want to grow—and grow effectively. Without these things, it's almost impossible to come face to face with Jesus. With them, it's possible to know Him, see why He's worth knowing, and experience the love, power, and beauty that make encountering Him the most important thing you'll ever do.

Many of the original Boy With a Ball team had seen their own difficult lives transformed by Jesus. They had experienced His love and power and how, when He entered into their world, everything changed. Yet they also witnessed the fact that churches were struggling to reach their own young people, let alone to reach out to their city's hardest-to-reach neighborhoods. Boy With a Ball's founding leaders saw this as a crisis: If the bad guys are more present and effective in our communities than the good guys at reaching and developing youth, our future is at risk. Something had to be done.

Around this time, one of the team members had a three-year-old boy who carried around a red kick ball with him wherever he went. The boy slept with the ball, took the ball to church with him, and even made his family drive 20 minutes back to the house to get the ball when he forgot to bring it with him on a family vacation. One day, the family went outside to play basketball and the boy placed his ball down next to the court while they played. As they finished and headed inside to cool down and get a drink, his ball fell out of his hands and bounced across the living room floor to his dad.

His dad thought, "I wonder if he can catch this ball if I bounce it to him?" and proceeded to bounce it to the boy. The boy caught it. The little boy threw the ball back to his dad, beginning his first ever game of catch. Instantly, a light went off in the boy's head as he thought: "I have been carrying this ball around for more than a year and I had no idea it (or I) could do this!" Boy With a Ball's name came from this story, realizing that young people need developmental relationships—positive, caring relationships with people who can whisper into their hearts and lives to teach them how to throw their lives into the hands of God their Father to see what He will throw back.

Over the last twenty-plus years, Boy With a Ball has grown from San Antonio, Texas to working in Central America, Africa, the Middle East, and other U.S. cities. In each city, we have encountered similar challenges: Young people are the secret to a city's future but are often reached most effectively by those who will hurt them. By working with young people in city after city all across the world, we found something: Young people are hungry to know Jesus personally and to then follow Him into the dreams He placed deep within their hearts. In order to do this, they desperately need to be equipped in the five **forgotten pieces** described in this book. These pieces are "forgotten" because they are found all across Scripture but yet sadly are rarely included in our approaches to drawing young people to faith.

We have found without exception that in every slum and at-risk neighborhood in every city in every country we have worked in all across the globe, young people are not only drawn to these pieces but are also transformed by them. Beyond that, young people who are given the opportunity to grow in these five things not only continue in their faith throughout the rest of their lives and also become leaders who walk with Jesus into "turning the world upside down" in neighborhood after neighborhood.

You may be someone who finds religious things distasteful, having turned away from the things of God because of the way people have demonstrated them to you. You may be someone who grew up in church and are familiar with these words and ideas. You may have even experienced something of these **Forgotten Pieces** in your walk with faith. Regardless of who you are, we believe you have chosen this book because you're looking for something that we, the authors, have spent years of our life in search of too.

We know the intense desire to live a life that matters, while cycling through the same strategies and ideas we've always had. We know what it's like to need to experience more than what we are currently experiencing in our lives. We know we often achieve the opposite of the very things we want to do (great, helpful, effective, hopeful, life-giving things). Of course, we know it's only Jesus who remakes, transforms, and satiates our hearts—but how does that happen?

These five **Forgotten Pieces** are tools that have changed our lives as we pursue Him. Time and time again, we've seen the effectiveness and essential nature of each of them. We have seen them lead us into a lifestyle that has impacted thousands of others. What is on the following pages is intended to help you too. May these pages confirm and strengthen you in what you have already experienced. May they encourage you to go deeper, and may they equip you to turn and help others around you to join you on this journey.

And so, let's begin.

Jamie Johnson
Atlanta, Georgia USA
June 2023

THREE TOOLS YOU WILL NEED

Twenty years of helping leaders across the world grow has taught us that you will need three tools in order to make the five *Forgotten Pieces* effective parts of your life. These tools are critical to your success (and that is an understatement).

In truth, there is no way forward without these three tools. You certainly can read on, but you will not be able to go on. The words on the following pages will only come to life if you take a moment, lay this book down, and secure these things. You will need:

1. **A Coach.** Like Morpheus in the movie, *The Matrix,*[2] or Mr. Beaver in C.S. Lewis's classic children's book, *The Lion, the Witch, and the Wardrobe,*[3] to get where you're going, you'll need to find someone else who has traversed this same terrain in order to help you do the same. Be careful here; not just anyone will do. There are many impressive individuals who talk about God and many who would like to lead you, but the majority of these people know nothing of the earnest journey you need and will so powerfully experience.

   Remember that while you will need a coach, it's not any coach in and of themselves you are after but the God who is after you. His power is such that He could make good use of even a bad coach to help you. Still, do everything you can to find a coach who will tell you stories of their search—stories that fill your heart with a dynamic hope as you listen.

   It's worth noting that you may find a coach who helps you initially, but then fades when a different person begins to prove to be more helpful to your growth. That is great and certainly part of the process of these **forgotten pieces** becoming more effective in your life.

   Your coach will invite you into their life to witness and touch how they have grown and how they live out these aspects of knowing and following Jesus. They will turn with you to Scripture to study how the characters in the Bible did the same. They will help you identify half-truths or false ideas about life that you've held onto for years but that are blocking your growth. Then they will also help you as these things reveal places where you have been hurt so you can turn to Jesus and ask Him for healing. Finally, they can go with you as you put these things into practice in life, work, and ministry.

Find a coach who lives the **forgotten pieces** in this book, using the three tools listed here on an active, moment-to-moment basis. Ask God to lead you to a qualified coach who won't just talk to you about these things but who will walk with you, work with you, and wrestle with you until your own life requires that you coach someone else in their pursuit of the same.

2. **A Team.** Just having a coach, however, would make the focus of your process too much about you. Therefore, it's vital that you go beyond finding a coach to being part of a team of individuals who are looking to grow in these five things as well. This could be a group of committed friends or a youth, college, or home group who will go after these things with you. Your team should be as committed to pursue Jesus and the pursuit of these five pieces as you. They'll make it easier and faster for you to grow as their growth and experiences push and provoke you—and vice versa.

Growing alone is the slowest, least reliable way to do so. When you're alone in all of this, it's easy for your faith to leak and form puddles on the floor. Alone, it's easy to be seduced by self-aggrandizing thoughts, believing you've really accomplished something. When you have a team, the relentless, sincere pursuit of others around you will continuously challenge your own pace. This group will support you and become eyewitnesses of your journey, reminding you of high and low points as necessary to keep you pushing forward.

3. **A Playing Field.** Finally, these tools require a place or "playing field" where you can practice and put them into action. No one learns to play the flute without a flute or to grow flowers without a flowerbed. No one learns to master skills without a place to put them into practice. This pursuit you're on isn't a philosophy class but a search to find, know, and love a real God who can be found, known, and loved and who Himself is actively involved. He's a God who is intimately involved in each piece of your everyday life, and it's in the actual, day-to-day, ordinary living where you will encounter Him and, in doing so, find these **forgotten pieces** you are looking for.

You will need to learn to recognize your whole life as your playing field, and you may even see the places you give your time shift as you grow to know the Lord more and learn His purpose for your life. You'll recognize that the people and places surrounding you are on purpose for His purpose. You'll learn that He wants to use you. And it is only in these places that you will get the practice you need to build the faith muscles required to live a life of real, substantive consequence.

You can (and should) use your school, workplace, or your neighborhood as a playing field in order to connect with people's hearts and lead them toward Jesus. Going together into a hurting neighborhood works well, too. Boy With a Ball designed our "Love Your City" program as such—a playing field for the young leaders we work with to create a space where they go into economically-disadvantaged neighborhoods to build relationships with the residents. As they go out in teams of two or three, they work on learning how to hear God's voice and follow His presence. They learn how to walk into and through uncomfortable situations to be led by the power of the Holy Spirit to see His miraculous help. Sometimes God will lead them to say something or stay quiet, to skip one door or go to one person, the result of which is a supernatural connection that changes both that person's life and their own.

Wherever your playing field is, recognize that it's important. You can't live an anonymous work life; you won't be able to ignore your neighbors. The places in which the Lord has called you to live and work are the places that He wants to use to teach you to effectively impact the lives of others.

Listening to His voice and direction in each playing field of life will lead to powerful moments; this is what it means to live a life of Spirit-led ministry. These five things grow most dynamically as you step into it and, as you do, you'll see God provide more and more clues about His purpose for your life.

As you are just beginning, it can be difficult to find a coach, team, and playing field or to know you've found the right ones. If you have never heard of these things, how will you find someone who lives out the **forgotten pieces** and will coach you, too? Even if you have people around, are they the right ones? Will they even want to team with you in this journey? There are many places you *could* impact people. How will you know you're not wasting your time?

It's okay if it takes time to find the right coach, team, and playing field. It's okay if the coach you have in the beginning is not the same in two years or in ten. Your team will grow and shift, some will decide that this process requires too much, some who are the most unexpected teammates will become those you depend on the most. You may be required to change your job, your address, or even your city in order to obey His voice and fulfill His purpose. The nature of the **forgotten pieces** is that they will lead you into a deep relationship with the God who will change your whole life. But don't let that scare you. We can confidently say that it will be worth it.

As your pursuit of the **forgotten pieces** intensifies, so will your relationship with these tools. You won't be able to hear and obey His voice, live in intimacy with Him, live by faith even when there's pain, find and fulfill His purpose for your life, or live in the power of the Holy Spirit without a coach, a team, and a playing field. Be open to the fact the Lord does provide everything you need, but He doesn't do so according to what you expect. Ask Him for the coach who will have eyes to see you and faith to believe in you. Ask Him to lead you to others who want to grow alongside you. Ask Him to tell you where He wants you to give your life. Ask and He will answer you. Make sure you're listening.

Now that you know the tools you'll need, you're ready to begin learning about the five **forgotten pieces**. These things were used by Jesus in His high-impact, miraculous, three-year ministry and have since been forgotten by many who claim to follow Him. This disconnection has led to many leaving the church, an inability to reach the next generation, and a complete separation of Christians from the miraculous power of God, among other things.

The return of the **forgotten pieces** in your life will lead you into an epic adventure, into intimacy with Him, as well as into purpose, help, and health. They will change you, your family, your church, your workplace, your friendships, your neighborhood, and, we believe, the world.

The First Forgotten Piece

LEARNING TO HEAR AND OBEY GOD'S VOICE

*"My sheep listen to my voice;
I know them, and they follow me"*
(John 10:27).

CHAPTER ONE

SAMUEL: ONE WHO HEARD

Throughout the Bible, all the greats heard God's voice. They talked with Him, and He responded. Sometimes He even initiated the conversation. And anyone who got hold of His purposes and plans did so because they heard His voice.

Abraham heard Him speak progressively about purpose. Moses heard Him speak on behalf of His people. Jesus only said what He heard the Father saying. Paul's life was interrupted and forever transformed by the boom of His voice. All these examples prove that God speaks constantly. He speaks faithfully. And He speaks to all of us.

Of course, it takes time and the miraculous work of the Holy Spirit to learn to hear Him, discern His voice from others, and obey. But that's part of the work of pursuing the Lord. We see this play out for one of the young heroes in the Bible—Samuel, who heard God's voice while he did not yet know Him (see 1 Samuel 3:7).

Sent away as a child to live in a church. Surrounded by spoiled, crooked pastor's and their kids. Far away from his mom. And living in a time, when, according to 1 Samuel

3:1, "The word of the Lord was rare." Young Samuel was living in a place where love was in short supply and change seemed far away.

Yet Samuel's lonely situation changed dramatically be-cause one night, while lying down to sleep, he heard God's voice.

Never having heard it before and living in the midst of a people who were unaccustomed to hearing God speak to them, Samuel understandably assumed the voice he heard was that of Eli the priest. So, he did what anyone does when someone calls to them; he called back.

"Here I am," Samuel said, but Eli didn't answer.

So Samuel went to the place where Eli usually slept.

"Here I am," said the boy, "you called me."

Eli, bothered in the middle of the night, didn't know what Samuel was talking about. "It wasn't me, kid. Go back to sleep."

Settling back down into his bed, enveloped again in the quiet of the black night, God spoke once more.

The voice the young man heard was audible, clear, and strong enough to cause him to go back to Eli again, having already been rebuked once, but convinced it must have been the priest who called him.

Eli was probably gruff, even more annoyed than before, as he denied calling Samuel this second time, turning him away once again. The words "go back to sleep" had to be ringing in Samuel's ears as he returned to his bed once more.

Scripture doesn't tell us what was running through Samuel's head and heart that night. Was he in a broken, desperate place? Was his heart crying out to God? The sto-ry does tell us that Samuel "did not yet know the Lord. The word of the Lord had not yet been revealed to him" (1 Samuel 3:7). From this, we're given a window into a life-changing, course-altering moment, not just for Samuel, but through him for an entire generation. For some reason, Samuel was chosen by God at this exact time to learn to hear, recognize, and respond to God's voice. Flipping back a few pages in our Bible, we see how God uniquely prepared Samuel for this moment.

In a faithless time when people were disconnected from God, Samuel understood better than most the power of crying out to God. His very existence was the result of his mother Hannah's passionate heart crying out to God asking for a baby (see 1 Samuel 1:9-11). Hannah vowed that if God would give her a son, she would give him back to God. So when Samuel was born, she took him to Eli to fulfill the promise she had made.

In a way that no other boy could have, Samuel understood the power of conversing with Yahweh. His whole life was a result of that having happened.

And so, when the voice came a third time, something grew in Samuel. Rather than being scared of bothering the priest yet again, he walked in boldly to respond to what he had heard.

Finally, the priest figured it out: "Then Eli realized that the Lord was calling the boy. So Eli told Samuel, 'Go and lie down, and if he calls you, say, 'Speak, Lord, for your servant is listening.' So Samuel went and lay down in his place" (1 Samuel 3:9).

Samuel went on to be a prophet and a fair judge over Israel. He served Saul and David in their reigns as kings. He was a man who knew God and who God used time and time again. And it all began with hearing God's voice.

Many people talk about God and even build their lives around religion—an idea that God exists and a general notion that because He lives, they are supposed to do good things. Yet time and again, this pursuit of a general faith practice fails, and the issue comes down to whether or not they actually *know* God. There simply is no way to know anyone without being able to communicate with them.

For many, this idea that God speaks is revolutionary, for others dangerous and heretical. But if it's possible, just think of what it means: You can converse with the God of the universe, hearing Him and sharing your voice with Him, too. You would have a direct line to the God who knows *everything*.

For Samuel, this was certainly a pivotal moment. He heard from God in a time when the voice of the Lord was rare and went on from there to be a mouthpiece for God—sharing His word and demonstrating obedience to His voice until he died.

Learning to hear and obey God's voice aren't magical or

9

tricky. He's always speaking. He wants to talk to you. He wants you to know His will if He expects you to do it. Every great man and woman in the Bible relied on hearing Him and were led by what He said. What it requires of us is acknowledging first that He does in fact speak, and then asking Him to help us hear.

Once we begin hearing God's voice and build up the faith to respond or obey, we step out in faith, trusting that responding to His voice will bring good results and bring us into things we would not get to listening to ourselves. God tells us to do something or to not do something and by doing it, we're given a chance to grow and go deeper into our relationship together. We learn we can trust Him. We may start with small steps of faith, like choosing to build a friendship with someone we know is further along in knowing Him so they can help us grow. Over time, we may take a bigger step—trying something that could be embarrassing if we've heard wrong.

The writer of Hebrews captures God's love for this way of growing faith and relationships with us by saying, "And it is impossible to please God without faith. Anyone who wants to come to him must believe that God exists and that he rewards those who sincerely seek him" (Hebrews 11:6). With each step of faith, we learn to hear His voice more clearly, to know how to confirm that what we have heard is really Him, and also learn that His word and promises are true and can be counted on.

As we hear His voice and respond, and as we share our thoughts and heart with Him, we begin learning about who God is. He's most often not at all what we expect. In the book of Isaiah, God explains this to us: "'For my thoughts are not your thoughts, neither are your ways my ways,' declares the Lord. 'As the heavens are higher than the earth, so are my ways higher than your ways and my thoughts than your thoughts'" (Isaiah 55:8-9). His words, what He cares about, and the way He does things are on one hand quite normal and easy to grasp. On the other hand, we're sometimes confronted with elements of who He is that leave our jaw on the floor, amazed by His love, power, and wisdom.

Slowly, His words begin to define our lives and our way of seeing things begins to reflect who He is. We become more and more like Him, while He is also listening and responding to our words or prayers. He is effective at building and deepening relationships, better than any friend we have ever encountered in our lives. Every promise and resulting experience deepens our faith, expands our relationship with Him, and transforms our lives. And then His power and His never-ending compassion flow from our hearts outward, empowering us touch the lives others.

Learning to hear and obey God's voice is a forgotten practice, even though we see it again and again in the Bible. It's forgotten because it's difficult and takes time to tune our hearts to hear. It requires us to diminish the importance of listening to our own voice, to know how to reject the voice of the enemy, and to treasure and act on any small thing we hear from God. It can be difficult at first, but it becomes easier with experience.

Like relating to a friend, you'll learn what He would and wouldn't say, and your faith will grow to accept that He will help you obey each time you step out. In the next chapters, you'll read real-life stories and the practical why and how-to's of learning to hear and obey God's voice. The best way to begin is to believe that He's constantly speaking, that He wants to speak directly with you, and that what He says will help you and change your life forever. Are you listening?

CHAPTER 2

A GLIMPSE AT LEARNING TO HEAR AND OBEY GOD'S VOICE

I still remember the pastor's words as we drove up to a car wash: "I was speaking at a university to a group in the open area of the campus and I heard God tell me, 'Someone in the crowd has a headache.' So I stopped my talk and asked, 'Hey, does anyone here have a headache? If you do, I want to pray for you, and I believe God wants to heal you.'" No one responded to him. Then, God spoke again. He asked the crowd a second time, but again, nothing.

A little later, a young woman came up to him crying. It was her head that was hurting. They prayed and God healed not only her head, but her heart. She learned that day how much God was paying attention to her life, how powerful He is, and to what extent He would go to help her. This small but supernatural story hit me like a wave. Throughout my life, my own dad, an alcoholic, had been out of reach, hiding behind his bedroom door or a drink. Yet there I was, learning that the most perfect Father in the world actually speaks to His children.

This story's impact on me that afternoon makes more sense when you learn that I was a 16-year-old atheist who, up to two weeks before that day, had hated the very idea of God. Fourteen days earlier, with tears streaming down my face, a knife in my hand and my life in ruins, I did what would have been unthinkable to me at any other point: I prayed. Instead of ending my life that night, I fell asleep.

The next day, the presence of God overwhelmingly filled the classroom where I was taking an algebra II/trigonometry final, and I experienced love, peace, and joy for the first time. I walked away from that test knowing God was real but not knowing who He was or what it meant. Miraculously, days later while driving with a pastor I had just met, I found out that the God who I now knew wanted to speak to me.

I would love to say that I heard Him that first day, but I didn't. In fact, I didn't hear directly from Him for two years. I first began hearing Him through the Bible the pastor had given me, through the messages he spoke each Sunday, and through people sharing things with me they sensed God was saying to me. For hours each week, I locked myself in my bedroom to ask Him to teach me to hear Him. While it took a very long time before He finally spoke directly to me, I could sense very clearly that I was moving closer and closer.

A few months later, I began to hear Him through bumper stickers and song lyrics, billboards, and even scenes from movies. The fact that this pursuit took two years forced me to make certain that I had done everything possible to allow it to happen. I met weekly with the pastor to learn and grow and to give me hints of how to hear, while sharing with me what God said to him. I found my place in a strong home group and youth group where I could learn from others trying to do the same thing.

Whatever I could do to grow, I did. With each day, I could sense God was recalibrating my heart, tuning me in to hear a voice that was speaking but that I didn't recognize. And then He spoke to my heart just the way my own thoughts could speak inside of my head. Something happened in my heart with each word. I sensed His presence and knew these words were not my own.

CHAPTER 3

WHY LEARN TO HEAR AND RESPOND TO GOD'S VOICE?

So, God speaks. But why does it matter? What does it mean for you that He has something to say? Well, He's the creator of the universe. He's your good Father. He knew you before time began, and He laid out your purpose alongside the foundation of the universe. He loves you—so much so that He would send His perfect Son to suffer and die because of the choices you made to turn away from Him and live a life less than what you were made for. He knows what will happen tomorrow and ten years from tomorrow. He knows who you will marry, the cares of your heart, and the one thing in the world you were made for.

To put it simply, His is the one voice you definitely want to hear. There are no words so important as the ones He has to say, and obeying what He says, even when it's difficult or you don't understand why, will heal every hurt in your heart and lead you into an adventurous, high-impact life—better, fuller, and more effective than anything you could imagine.

The following are six very real, very practical reasons why you need to learn to hear and respond to God's voice.

1. You receive direction connected to deeper wisdom.

Every situation you face confronts you with variables—some you see and some you don't. You see a small part of the larger picture but have little to no control over the wide range of factors involved in a single instance of your life. We see this play out all the time in the world around us: A cautious, attentive driver responds to every rule of the road, only to be struck on the side by a distracted individual who runs a red light. A high-performance athlete develops to the point where nothing can stop them only to suffer a major injury in practice. Someone has time to study 80% of the course curriculum only to discover that the test centers on the 20% they neglected.

Yet even apart from missed threats, the difficulty of seeing every opportunity for good is far more overwhelming and difficult to do. In every second of every day, you face an infinite number of possibilities where amazing things could occur. A word could be spoken to unlock a person's heart; a person who is hurting could be helped; something could be discovered, built, or accomplished that could change our lives, the life of another, or even the world. But how do you see these things? How do you know when they're in front of you? How do you know what to do?

God uses every part of your life to wake you up and draw you to Him, and He is present everywhere, aware of all things. Beyond that, He is sovereign or, said differently, He is able to work all things together for good (see Romans 8:28). When you learn to hear God's voice, He can lift you out of your significant limitations, giving you direction to navigate each moment of life—even the most challenging ones. Without His voice in your life, Jesus compared you to sheep without a shepherd, harassed and helpless (see Matthew 9:36). With His voice, you receive words telling you what you need to know and light revealing what you need to see so that in every way you get in on what you are supposed to. Jesus, as the Good Shepherd, leads you into everything you need, protects you from every bad thing, and helps you realize the deep desires of your heart.

2. His voice gives you access to His comfort and love.

Most people's lives are built around seeking consolation, comfort, or peace in the midst of storms of angst, discomfort, and trouble. We sense something is missing and so we eat, drink, watch, touch, worry, and purchase things to make us feel better. When these things don't do the trick, we turn to look for more or for something else. The life of the average person isn't spent relating to others, but instead self-medicating.

You are drawn to this God who pursues you because you correctly sense that He isn't subject to these same storms. There's a strength to Him, a peace, that you don't have but that you get a taste of when you experience God's presence in any way.

The pain in your soul is actually an aching for His voice. God created you by speaking you into existence. The Father grabs dust from the ground, breathes into it or speaks into it, and it is made alive. His breath or voice is the animating force. And then, He made you not to live by bread alone but by every word that comes out of God's mouth (see Deuteronomy 8:3 and Matthew 4:4).

3. You are reconnected to living the way you were made.

In Genesis, we learn that when the enemy comes to attempt to kill and destroy us, he very cunningly attacks the source of our life: he attacks our capacity to hear and obey God's voice. "Did God really say...?" Satan asked this again and again until Adam and Eve became disoriented enough to do something they had never done before; they ignored God's words to them (see Genesis 3). The death they died spiritually continues on in every person we know until God moves in on these spiritually blind and deaf humans (like you and me) to get them to open their hearts to Him. When we do respond to His pursuit, however weakly, His Word comes into our hearts again, just as it did back in the Garden. We are born again, and everything changes.

Recovering from this death is a process. In the midst of your spiritual death which creates that deep pain inside you, you've learned to seek consolations, substitutes to alleviate the pain. Even now that you are spiritually alive you must learn to abandon old habits while learning to enjoy Him, hear His voice, and allow it to reconstruct, renew, and make you whole again.

His voice comes in the midst of the worst storms and calms them. His voice comes into the darkest problems and gives light to follow Him to a better place. His voice tells you who you are and who He is, and teaches you how to relate to Him and to others. His voice says again and again that He loves you, that you don't need to be afraid any longer. His voice tells you that you're forgiven, accepted, right with Him, and it promises you very specific things for your future. These promises provide hope and a way forward that includes growing closer both to Him and His love.

4. You receive the Lord's wisdom in facing the circumstances of your life.

We know wisdom when we see it. A kind older person seems to move at a different pace than the world around them. They somehow exist outside of the cares of this world. It's as if they have something that can't be given or taken away. It's as if they know something that transcends the moment—experts in their field, war veterans, astronauts, even young people with a unique talent seem to see things in their area of proficiency that others cannot. And then there are leaders. True leaders have an awareness of how to face any given situation in a way that leads forward.

Jesus demonstrates this on a different level. He knows people's thoughts. He reads their hearts and understands their motives in a way that leads to their lives being changed. He responds to traps laid for Him like a person walking through a minefield with a map in their hands. He knows exactly what to say, what not to say, where to go, and when to walk away. All these things leave us awestruck and draw us to come closer. Yet, there's something deeper here in Jesus. He doesn't just interact with profound insight but He accesses wisdom and understanding in a way that doesn't just make a moment; it solves existential problems for each one of us.

By learning to hear God's voice, you begin a continuous conversation with the One who not only has wisdom but *is* Wisdom. This isn't the kind of stuff you download and grasp at any one time. By trusting His voice, He leads you to do things no one would ever do and for seemingly good reasons. One step after another, Jesus takes you along a pathway that could never work, gets you in some trouble, and leaves everyone around you– including you–questioning whether you really heard His voice at all.

And then it works. And not only does it work in the way you first perceived it, but you begin to see that He is leading you into participating in His eternal purposes. You are being woven into His mission to bring all things under His feet (see 1 Corinthians 15:27), to make all things right (see Isaiah 42:1), to help every helpless person to find their way home to Him (see Mark 2:17).

5. You get access to His power in your life.

For those of us who Jesus is awakening and drawing to Him, power is pretty far down on the list of what we're after. After all, we are those who haven't found traction in a world that doesn't satisfy or help us. What good would power do?

Yet the thing that draws you to God is the sense that things can and will change if you get closer to Him. We live in a world of many words and messages, new gimmicks and gadgets, but nothing changes. Apart from rare exceptions, poor people stay poor. Wealthy people continue to be consumed by what they have. Marriages don't last. Broken people from broken families raise up broken children. When faced with all this, it's easy to feel helpless.

This Jesus who wants to speak to you is powerful and the more you learn to hear Him, follow Him, and stay close to Him, the more your life comes into more and regular contact with His power. You're invited to a front row seat to experience who God is and what He does. This God who relates, who loves, who creates, is a Father who so loves people that He sends His only Son to rescue us (see John 3:16). This Son, Jesus, lives in a way that shows us everything we have lost in walking away from His voice all those years ago in the Garden. We learn what it is to hear the Father's voice by the way that Jesus lives in response to that voice and it introduces miraculous power into your life.

6. You get a relationship with Jesus.

The greatest gift in all of these things is that we get a relationship with the God who has been pulling us toward Him. We get life as it is meant to be: His life flowing in and through us to affect other people's lives.

In learning to hear God's voice, you come to know Him more and more deeply. With every word He says, you begin to see more clearly that His words are true and trustworthy. You learn that He says and does things very differently than the world around you. You learn that He often says things or make promises that go directly against the circumstances you face and what you see, feel, or hear from others. Yet you also learn that what He says works, while every other philosophy, best practice, or trend is temporary and cannot be counted on. You learn to trust His voice.

As we do all this, our lives start to fill with the kind of miraculous stories that His life was filled with. We find ourselves repeatedly in the right place at the right time to help others, not with anything we can do but with His power, love, and wisdom directing us. We begin to get in on His promise that we'll do even greater things (see John 14:12) than He did in His three-year ministry. And we become His friends (see John 15:15).

When you don't hear His voice, you miss out on an entire part of your relationship with Him. Hearing and obeying His voice causes you to relate to Him in an interactive way. It enables you to know what you should do, how you should respond, and how you can best impact the lives of others in real time. Hearing Him keeps you from wasting time or stepping into a fight that you aren't called to. His voice is the only good and wise voice, and you'll uncover a never-ending list of the reasons why you need to hear it.

CHAPTER 4

HOW TO HEAR AND OBEY GOD'S VOICE

It's one thing to *want* to hear Him; it's an entirely different thing to know *how*. Like a young child learning to crawl, then walk, then run, so it is with this **forgotten piece**. Because it hasn't been an active practice for you, you'll likely not hear full paragraphs; you're much more likely to hear one word or a short phrase in the beginning. Respond to what you do hear, because it will build faith for the days where you hear sentences, paragraphs, and novels of His words. How does it work? Where do you begin? The following are seven practical ways to begin (and continue) to hear God's voice.

1. Listen with your heart, not your ears.

"God is a spirit; and they that adore Him, must adore Him in spirit and in truth" (John 4:24). While God can speak audibly and does so across the pages of Scripture, we most often hear Him in our hearts. It is in our thought lives that we actually hear three voices: our own, the enemy's, and God's. Our own voice is pretty easy to separate out as we know the kind of things that we would usually think or say.

The enemy's voice can come from many different angles:

accusing or condemning you, seducing you into temptation, or puffing you up with proud thoughts. However, a good test to identify Satan's words is that, whether they appear to be positive or negative, you are discouraged, fearful, or anxious after hearing them. When God speaks to you, even though you hear it inaudibly and it can closely resemble a thought, you also sense hope in your heart. The words resonate with you, and they lift you to a higher place. They will even inspire you.

2. Grab a Bible.

The Bible becomes a different kind of book when you begin to give yourself to learning to hear God's voice. First, you begin to see God speaking to people on every page. However, you can also learn to read the Bible differently, less intent on trying to read from start to finish or to memorize certain verses. Instead, you can focus on reading through passages in search of where the words on the page begin to come alive in your heart. Reading the Bible this way has a two-fold effect.

First, it's one way to begin hearing God's voice. Take note of which verses impact your heart and learn to respond to these words because they're God's voice. From this point, hearing God's voice directly becomes second nature. Second, the more you read Scripture, the more you know who God is and the kind of things He says. When you do begin to hear His voice, it's much easier to know whether what you are hearing is His voice and not your own or the enemy's.

3. Keep a journal.

The process of learning to hear God speak through Scripture opens up the realization that God is constantly speaking and you can learn to hear Him in every moment of your life. Purchase a notebook or journal or create a document on your phone, and stay open to all of the different mediums through which God can speak. Listen for words in songs that bring tears to your eyes or grab your heart. Listen for the same in lines from movie scenes. Look for words spoken in sermons or through members of your small groups that resonate in your heart. Be aware that

God can speak through bumper stickers, billboards, words said in conversations, or even famous quotes. If you sense something in any of these things, take a minute to write them down in your journal alongside verses from the Bible.

4. Learn to confirm what He might be saying through Scripture, your coach, and your team.

This process teaches you an important lesson in learning to hear God's voice. It's one thing to hear Him. It's another thing entirely to know for sure that you've heard Him. Remember, your challenge isn't just to hear what God is saying but to respond to it with action. This is called obedience. If you were just trying to write down a few thoughts from God to show others, confirming that you have actually heard Him would be less critical. However, when you hear Him with the idea of learning to turn and step into it, you need to know you're actually hearing from Him.

In the early stages of trying to discern His voice, it's critical to run what you hear by your coach. Bring your notebook, share the recurring patterns you notice in what you write down, and be willing to openly share everything you might be hearing so they can help you confirm or deny it. This way, you won't waste time on things God did not say to you. Your coach can help take the beginnings of what God might be saying and confirm you're on the right track. As you go further, your coach and team will also help to hold you accountable for stepping out to actually respond to what you're hearing.

5. Respond quickly to what you hear.

As you get better at confirming what God says to you with a coach and a team, your focus will move from hearing God's word to doing it. Keep this in mind: If God is constantly speaking and you're to be constantly obeying what He says to you, there will simply be no way to take everything you hear back to your coach or team for confirmation. It's important to meet regularly with your accountability partners to share the kind of things you're hearing or major decisions God is speaking to you about for help. However, the goal of the process is for you to grow strong enough in hearing His voice so that you can respond moment to moment, even when you have no time to run it by anyone. Hearing and obeying, hearing and obeying— may this become the rhythm of your life.

6. Continually tune yourself in.

Even with the Holy Spirit within us, it's important to remember that "we have this treasure in jars of clay" (2 Corinthians 4:7). We're fragile, sensitive, and imperfect people living in a world with an enemy who is constantly at our heels. Pride and momentum are a sure way to knock off even the most mature and experienced follower of Jesus. It's because of this fragility that investing ourselves in spiritual disciplines like prayer, reading the Bible, being a part of a local church, and having accountability like a coach and a team are so important.

These rhythms of mutual accountability and iron sharpening iron (see Proverbs 27:17) keep our hearts clean, clear, and tuned in to be able to hear God clearly and to respond earnestly. What's more, a person who is being directed by God's voice is a tremendous threat to the enemy, and he will do whatever he can to take that person out. This isn't something we grow out of, and it's something that becomes more and more important as we live our lives in response to His voice.

7. Work towards a constant conversation.

The goal of learning to hear and obey God's voice is to grow into a closer and closer relationship with Jesus. This means that your life must be lived in a constant, deepening conversation with Him. Hearing and responding to God's voice throughout every part of your day makes you like a guided missile that knows how to handle every situation because you are connected to God's love and purpose.

While many people fear that their lives will be destroyed by a sudden disaster or wonder whether they're in the right job, marrying the right person, or making the right choices, you won't have to wonder because you'll know for certain that you're right where you're supposed to be. You'll know this because you'll have heard God tell you. Even more, you'll be able to continually turn to the Lord and to share your concerns, fears, hopes, and desires with Him through-out your day. He will hear you, and He will help you.

You will learn as you hear His voice more and more that the Lord speaks all the time and in many different ways. Know this: Learning to hear His voice is a life-changing gift. It gives you access to deep wisdom, all truth, abundant guidance, and more. Listening for Him and obeying what He says should be the rhythm of your life. When it is, you'll experience a different, better, fuller way of living and you'll participate in important, miraculous things.

CHAPTER 5

LEARNING TO HEAR AND OBEY GOD'S VOICE: A SUMMARY

All the heroes in the Bible heard God speak. When He spoke, God shared purpose, hope, faith, and help with these men and women of faith. They were often just beginning to face circumstances too big for them to handle, or they were in a desperate place with broken hearts. When God spoke to them, their situations changed and they were transformed because of it. God's voice changes everything, and He speaks all the time. The problem is that we, with our broken, sin-filled hearts, are often too consumed with our own consolations to hear Him. We're out of shape and need His help to give us faith for the obedience to change.

When we do learn to hear His voice and obey, we have access to a new play book. All of a sudden, the God of the whole universe and everything in it is helping us by telling us our next step and revealing to us the places where we are broken. His words bring new life to our dead hearts and we grow. This first piece, learning to hear and obey God's voice, is forgotten because our sin disconnects us, and we aren't naturally inclined to hear Him. When it returns to us, we recover part of our relationship that's been missing. We then have His help and direction. He will speak to us about big, life-shifting things and about small, quiet details. His voice will change us, and we will love Him differently as we hear and obey it.

In this section, you read about Samuel, who heard God's voice in a time when the voice of the Lord was rare. We wrote about the reasons why and how you can learn to hear and obey God's voice.

Why learn to hear and respond to God's voice?

1. You receive direction connected to deeper wisdom.

2. His voice gives you access to His comfort and love.

3. You are reconnected to living the way you were made to.

4. You receive the Lord's wisdom in facing the circumstances of your life.

5. You get access to His power in your life.

6. You get a relationship with Jesus.

How do you hear God's voice?

1. Listen with your heart, not your ears.

2. Grab a bible.

3. Keep a journal.

4. Learn to confirm what He might be saying through Scripture, your coach, and your team.

5. Respond quickly to what you hear.

6. Continually tune yourself in.

7. Work towards a constant conversation.

Many don't realize that God speaks, much less learn to hear and obey Him. In the beginning, He will speak a word or two. Write them down and share them with your coach and team. Do whatever you can to obey Him. As you do, you'll learn more and more what His voice sounds like and how to discern the difference between His voice, your voice, and the voice of the enemy. His words are the only good and helpful ones. Learn to hear and obey His voice. Do everything you can with even the smallest things you hear, and watch as your life fills with vision, hope, and faith.

Forgotten Piece Two

LIVING IN MOMENT-TO-MOMENT INTIMACY WITH GOD

*"I am the vine; you are the branches.
If you remain in me and I in you,
you will bear much fruit; apart from me
you can do nothing"*
(John 15:5).

CHAPTER 6

THE APOSTLE JOHN: THE ONE JESUS LOVED

Our daily lives are lived within a constant and very noisy battle for our attention. Marketers come after us from every direction through billboards, commercials, magazine ads, bumper stickers, emails, and text messages. Media, including news and entertainment, work around the clock to grab viewers and never (they hope) let us go. Our work can't be left at the office because it continues to stream into our personal lives through our phones. It can even be difficult to hear someone's voice when you're with them because of there are so many other voices trying to distract and engage you.

The same is true when it comes to hearing God. In order to hear His voice, you have some work to do in clearing space to do so in your heart and mind. Worship is the choice you make to give your heart and being to something. In order to worship God, you are forced to turn away from everything else—this includes your own very busy thought life.

A.W. Tozer said, "We have as much of God as we actually want."[4] Throughout Scripture, we see people who come to know God and are then invited into encountering His presence, which transforms their own experience as well as impacts the lives of those around them. This treasure, the presence of God, changes our lives and the lives of anyone we touch. Learning to jettison the presence of distractions in us to cultivate a life in His presence is a key to knowing and following Jesus. If we are looking for how to live in intimate connection with God, we have few examples better than the apostle Jesus loved.

At the same time that Jesus began calling His disciples, which launched His three-year public ministry, an adolescent boy named John had already made a faith-soaked, passionate leap to follow another spiritual leader of that day.

Following John the Baptist wasn't for the faint of heart. His prophetic voice and lifestyle certainly captured the public's attention but didn't create a popular following. There was a cost to associate with a leader whose diet was locusts and honey and who was best known for his constant calls to repentance from the outskirts of society and religious life.

This teenager, John, was a disciple of John the Baptist. And though he had most likely not yet reached his sixteenth birthday, he was mature and strong enough to spend his days on his father's fishing boat, alongside James, his older brother. John wasn't alone. Andrew and his brother, Peter, were James' and John's partners in the fishing business but Andrew and John were the ones who had made the bold decision to follow their deep spiritual hunger into "the Baptizer's" camp.

We get a sense of those two young men's hearts for God when they walk by Jesus and John the Baptist cries out, "Look, the Lamb of God!"

> When the two disciples heard him say this, they followed Jesus. Turning around, Jesus saw them following and asked, "What do you want?" They said, "Rabbi" (which means 'Teacher'), "where are you staying?" "Come," he replied, "and you

will see." So they went and saw where he was staying, and they spent that day with him (John 1:36-39).

And so begins one of the greatest stories of intimate friendship and of committed discipleship. John, the future apostle, becomes one of Jesus's first two disciples but, more importantly, shows us a depth of relational intimacy with Jesus that stands apart from the other eleven and that has inspired millions of people to seek the same over the last two millennia.

We know that thousands of people came into contact with Jesus. He walked through the multitudes of individuals who witnessed or participated in one of His miracles—like the day He miraculously multiplied a little boy's lunch box to feed 5,000 people as reported in Matthew 14:13-21.

Paul writes of a group that had built a closer relationship than these large crowds. In 1 Corinthians 15:6, we read, "After that, he appeared to more than five hundred of the brothers and sisters at the same time, most of whom are still living, though some have fallen asleep." Jesus did nothing without purpose in it. This means that Jesus had connected to or built some kind of relationship with these 500 people that made appearing to them impactful. So this group of 500 would seem to be one step closer than the rest of those who witnessed His miracles.

Closer still were the 120 individuals who, after Jesus had gone up to Heaven, waited, according to His command, to be filled with the Holy Spirit in the upstairs room (see Acts 1:15). There was an even smaller number that included the seventy-two individuals Jesus sent out two by two to practice what He had trained them to do (see Luke 10:1).

Now we get very close as we come to the twelve disciples whom Jesus chose, trained, and sent out. These twelve lived, slept, ate, learned, and ministered alongside Jesus for three-action packed years. This is a level of access that no one else had (Mark 3:14-17).

Even beyond the twelve, there were three—James, Peter and John—who were given a level of intimate access or relationship far deeper than the others. In repeated instances across the gospels, these three were given front-row seats

to witness what no one else did. An example of this includes the Mount of Transfiguration in Luke 9:18-36 where
Moses and Elijah joined Jesus in His prayer time, and God
spoke audibly from Heaven.

Beyond even the intimacy of the three, there was one
who was closer: John. It's interesting and makes sense that
John's gospel is the version with the clearest description
of Jesus's intimate relationship with the Father. John had
a yearning for intimacy with Jesus that allowed him to become known as "the disciple whom Jesus loved"—not because Jesus played favorites but because of John's capacity
to come close.

John was chosen as one of the twelve and then repeatedly drawn into the unique experiences of the three, alongside his brother, James, and their old fishing partner, Peter.
In John 13:22-24, as Jesus gathered His disciples for a last
supper before His death, John was seated next to Jesus
with his head laying on Jesus's chest. Over the next few
dramatic hours, all the other disciples would run away in
fear, including Peter, who denied Jesus three times. Yet in
the account of Jesus hanging on the cross, John was the
only disciple who was still there. What happened next was
almost impossible to comprehend:

> Near the cross of Jesus stood his mother, his
> mother's sister, Mary the wife of Clopas, and
> Mary Magdalene. When Jesus saw his mother
> there, and the disciple whom he loved stand-
> ing nearby, he said to her, "Woman, here is your
> son," and to the disciple, "Here is your mother."
> From that time on, this disciple took her into his
> home (John 19:25-27).

From the cross, Jesus looked down and asked John, His
beloved disciple, to care for His mother, Mary—a level of
closeness, friendship, and trust that is difficult to match.

There's a remarkable section of John's gospel, in John
21:20-23, where Jesus restored Peter after Peter's denial
of Him and yet, even in such a touching, rich moment of
experiencing God's mercy, Peter couldn't help being jealous
of John's relationship with Jesus:

> Peter turned and saw that the disciple whom

> Jesus loved was following them. (This was the
> one who had leaned back against Jesus at the
> supper and had said, 'Lord, who is going to
> betray you?') When Peter saw him, he asked,
> "Lord, what about him?" Jesus answered, 'If I
> want him to remain alive until I return, what is
> that to you? You must follow me.' Because of
> this, the rumor spread among the believers that
> this disciple would not die. But Jesus did not say
> that he would not die; he only said, 'If I want
> him to remain alive until I return, what is that to
> you?' (John 21:20-23).

This "rumor" that John would never die was due to the
level of intimacy He had found in His relationship with
Jesus, and it exemplifies how the disciples understood that
intimacy with Jesus could change a person's life. In the
Book of Martyrs, we catch a glimpse of John: «Among the
numerous martyrs that suffered during this persecution
was . . . St. John, who was boiled in oil and afterward ban-
ished to Patmos." Early Christian author Tertullian wrote
further on this in A.D. 200, describing how "at Rome, the
Apostle John, having been immersed in hot oil, suffered no
harm at all from it."

Long after Jesus's death and resurrection, John grew so
dangerous to those resisting the spread of Christianity that
the only way to slow his influence was to banish him to the
isle of Patmos. It's difficult to imagine a human being growing so close to God that their life is filled with such grace
and power that the only way to keep them from changing
the world is to isolate them hundreds of miles away from
others.

John's intimate friendship with Jesus is further evidenced
in Revelation 1:9-10. When Jesus was looking for someone
to write down how everything will end one day, the book of
Revelation, He decided to show up and share it with John.

However, perhaps the greatest testament to the closeness of John's relationship with Jesus is his gospel. The
Gospel of John gives more insight than any of the other
eyewitness accounts into what the King of kings, Lord of
lords, Savior of the world, and Son of God saw as most

valuable: His own almost unfathomable relationship of dependence on both the Father and also on the power of the Holy Spirit.

As we read the story of John, the beloved disciple, we have to wonder whether Jesus demonstrated favoritism to John. However, knowing Jesus was without sin, we're forced to grapple with the truth that John received more love from Jesus because he was so intentional about letting himself be loved by His Master. Like Mary, Martha's sister, John made it his focus to seek Jesus, to be with Jesus, to stay with Jesus, and to grow in trusting Jesus.

It's important to realize that John was, above all, a very good disciple. His life and pursuit of intimacy with Jesus were things he learned from Jesus. This was the way that Jesus Himself lived—in constant, intimate relationship with God, the Father, through the power of the Holy Spirit—and it was given to us by God as an invitation for our new way of life.

In the following chapters, you'll find stories, reasons why, and the beginning guide to living in moment-to-moment intimacy with God. This **forgotten piece** needs to return to our lives because those who live in intimacy with Him experience more of the One who overcomes every lack and breaks through every hurt. John is a powerful example of someone who took Jesus up on His offer, and today that same offer is extended to each of us. The question remains: How close will you come to the One who your heart yearns to be close to?

CHAPTER 7

A GLIMPSE OF LEARNING TO LIVE IN MOMENT-TO-MOMENT INTIMACY

"Tick. Tick. Tick. Tick," was the sound of my hand-me-down car with a hand-me-down engine on the hour-long drive to university each morning. I was a poor college student and my budget didn't have much room for unexpected or even anticipated expenses. The depleting gas tank and the rising temperature due to a faulty radiator both meant the car was going to cost money I didn't have. And now I heard the engine ticking.

Just before setting off for school each day, I would bow down next to my bed to try and learn to pray alone in my room. Being a new follower of Jesus, none of this came naturally. The moment I hit my knees to pray, my mind would either begin racing or I would fall asleep. I desperately fought both those tendencies so I could focus on Jesus, knowing what He had already done in my life in such a short time and eager to see Him do more. I needed Him to help me overcome my faithless, anxious, and distracted mind and heart.

On the days when a breakthrough would happen and I would sense His presence, my next challenge was not to let it wear off on the ride to school. Leaving my house with a strong sense of connection to Jesus, the battle was on: Could I keep my mind on Him even as traffic, school assignments, a virtually non-existent bank account, and an increasingly troubled car all confronted me moment by moment during my drive?

Even in the midst of such distractions, I could clearly sense that God was calling me closer. He was with me and ready to speak to me, to touch my heart, to help me, and to guide me. As my mind would turn to worrying or thinking through every possibility of how I could work things out, I could sense Him inviting me to lay those things down at His feet so I could be with Him.

For a few weeks, my wandering heart actually chose to reject this invitation by turning on Christian radio; I reasoned that the songs were at least about Him. Gradually, my heart was convicted but, stalling again, I would turn to listening to worship tapes, telling myself that these songs honored the God I was avoiding. Jesus stepped in to help me by breaking my car stereo. At last, I was out of distractions and was forced to confront my anxious heart. Could I quiet my thoughts and keep my heart interacting with the Creator of the universe who was somehow in my car, fighting for my attention?

Month after month, year after year, I tried every trick I could to train myself to "abide in Him." If I was knocked off the horse, forgetting that God even existed for a few hours, I would just repent, come back to Him, and start again. Little by little, His presence and love became more natural to me than my anxious, racing mind.

Years later, Jesus invited me to a simpler way: If I could just "get in the car with Him" at the beginning of my days and not choose to get out, He would keep me close. I imagine each of us is different and the battles we face to "take every thought captive" will be won in a myriad of different ways. It is possible, though, and critically important that we learn to stay in the car, rejecting the many voices and reasons we face trying to pull us out. He laid down His life to call us home, into an intimate relationship with the Father, His Son, Jesus, and the Holy Spirit. He will teach us to come close and stay close.

CHAPTER 8

WHY LIVE IN MOMENT-TO-MOMENT INTIMACY WITH GOD?

You want to live in moment-to-moment intimacy with God because He is good. He means good for you; He loves you wildly. What's more, He knows you better than anyone, including yourself. And then, the reasons build on that. Like any relationship, the time spent together is how you learn about Him. The more you are together, the more you understand God's ways. You learn what He sounds like. You experience moment by moment His pursuit of you and those in your life. You get access to His gifts, His help, His comfort. Every other **forgotten piece** is made exponentially easier by your ability to learn this one. Living a faith-filled, impactful life is made possible by learning to live this way. While there's no end to this list, the following are five reasons why we have found it critical to live your life in moment-to-moment intimacy with God.

1. You can hear God's voice continuously.

You learned in an earlier chapter that God speaks to you and wants to speak to you throughout your day—in every moment and in every decision. The opportunity to walk closely with Him, to know Him, and to be directed by Him through the complex things we face is a game changer. But, for some people, this reality is one they still struggle with even after knowing it's a possibility.

It's common for all of us to have a hard time remembering to listen to what God is saying because you get caught up in the circumstances, people, and emotions you experience in life. For hours of the day, you forget He is with you, and you don't allow yourself to wait for His voice because you're too caught up in the momentum of your day-to-day life. By learning to live in an awareness of God, continually connected to Him, you make it much easier to pay attention to and be expectant of what God is saying to you.

2. It's easier to obey when you do hear God speak.

While it's true that God is omnipresent and that His presence is with you constantly, it's also true that you can experience His "manifest presence," or instances where His presence can be physically sensed or experienced. As you grow in your ability to stay open and connected to God throughout your days, you create more room for the Holy Spirit to come into your daily life and normalize the experience of God's presence and power.

In these moments when you sense His presence and then hear Him speak, obedience to what He says is much easier because you are in the midst of experiencing His peace and provision. When your faith is low, your circumstances seem impossible, and every feeling and voice around you tells you what God is saying is crazy, it's difficult to step into obedience. Yet when God's presence comes flooding into these situations, you can actually feel that He is with you, and His presence displaces the fog with faith. As a result, you'll step out to do what He has told you to do.

3. You displace negative thoughts with joy.

Many people struggle to control their thoughts. Negative

and fearful thoughts, lust, obsessions, suspicions, fantasies, and an inability to concentrate or be present are just a few of the things that overwhelm people's minds as they go through their days. Many young people struggle to go to sleep at night because their thought lives grow into a raging fire, keeping them awake for hours. Learning to live in moment to moment intimacy with God, or practicing His presence, takes time. It doesn't happen in an instant.

Rather than trying not to think of something (which is an impossible task), it requires you to displace your attention from your ideas and instead give your attention to the God who is with you. You will learn to stay aware of Him throughout your day instead of drowning in yourself. The immediate reward is that the storms in your mind are quieted: "You will keep him in perfect peace, whose mind is stayed on You, because he trusts in You" (Isaiah 26:3). The word *joy* in Greek is the word *chara*, and means the awareness of God's grace or favor.

Joy is grace recognized or the ability to see that God is close to you and that He is for you. There's a difference between walking through your daily life consumed by negative, oppressive thoughts and keeping your mind and heart focused on God being with you, for you, and in love with you. The difference makes room for joy.

4. You will flourish, grow, and bear effective fruit.

Just a few days before the crucifixion, Jesus turned to His disciples and said,

> "I am the true vine, and my Father is the gardener. He cuts off every branch in me that bears no fruit, while every branch that does bear fruit he prunes so that it will be even more fruitful. You are already clean because of the word I have spoken to you. Remain in me, as I also remain in you. No branch can bear fruit by itself; it must remain in the vine. Neither can you bear fruit unless you remain in me" (John 15:1-4).

Here Jesus provides His closest followers with an instructive metaphor: Just as a branch receives nutrients from the vine to give it life necessary for it to grow, so we receive love, light, and life from staying connected to Jesus. If we "remain in Him, we will bear fruit." This fruit can be the close relationship, peace, and joy detailed above but it can also be our capacity to help other people around us. Jesus doesn't stop there:

> "I am the vine; you are the branches. If you re-main in me and I in you, you will bear much fruit; apart from me you can do nothing. If you do not remain in me, you are like a branch that is thrown away and withers; such branches are picked up, thrown into the fire and burned. If you remain in me and my words remain in you, ask whatever you wish, and it will be done for you. This is to my Father's glory, that you bear much fruit, showing yourselves to be my disci-ples. As the Father has loved me, so have I loved you. Now remain in my love. If you keep my commands, you will remain in my love, just as I have kept my Father's commands and remain in his love" (John 15:5-10).

"If you remain in me" is a phrase that Jesus repeated sev-eral times, encouraging and admonishing His disciples to listen to His words and to stay connected to Him through-out their lives. If they stay connected they would flourish, grow, and change many people's lives. If they did not, they would wither away and spiritually die. This is the power of living in moment-to-moment intimacy with Jesus. The closer to Him you live, the more you will produce effective and abundant fruit.

5. You become a person of His presence.

Intimacy with God isn't a nice add-on to an already good salvation. Intimacy with Him is the very way you were de-signed to live, and every other alternative, be it *some* inti-macy or none at all, is a worse life and an ineffective way. Outside of His presence, you are bound to the things of this world. You are oppressed by the restrictive ways of rules, judgment, expectations, and pace of the world. In His pres-ence, you are free from all that, equipped with access to

His constant provision, His voice, and the ability to follow Him in whatever He says.

After Jesus' crucifixion, He appeared to a group of 120 of His followers, teaching them about the Kingdom of God. He left them with one instruction: They could not go out. They had to wait for the gift God had promised—the gift of the Holy Spirit (see Acts 1:3-9). When that happened and they received the Holy Spirit, the miraculous, overwhelming power that raised Jesus from the dead, that overcame every curse and sin on Earth, resided *within* them. And they became different; they were transformed.

When you are a person of His presence, you're different. You're consistently in tune with Jesus ways and God's words. You're not bogged down in the ways of the world; you surf it, pulling others out of the tumultuous seas as you head toward His purpose. You have no need of fear of the unknown, of man, or of circumstances; you are constantly connected to the One who knows everything and is over everything. You know where your physical and spiritual provision come from. You are free to worship Him, concerned for nothing, while others have to console or bury their hurt by artificial, unnatural means, like making money, gorging on food, or buying bigger houses. As a person of His presence, you understand the deeper ways God works, and you're free from everything except the desperate, satisfying offer of living every moment close to Him. Becoming a person of His presence is what you were made for, and moment-to-moment intimacy with Him is the way that leads you to that reality.

The more you're with Him, the more you'll love Him. And the more you love Him, the more you will yearn to be with Him. When you *know* the Lord and stay with Him throughout your day, you're transformed because of Who you're with. The reasons to live your life this way are numerous. Like any great relationship, you'll constantly uncover more and more of who the Lord is and as you do, your life will change and you'll grow because of it.

CHAPTER 9

HOW TO LIVE IN MOMENT- TO-MOMENT INTIMACY WITH GOD

When you forget He is with you, you lose access to your help and the guide for your life. You miss opportunities to be with Him. You don't see miraculous change, and you're forced to depend on your best efforts (which don't work). Living in moment-to-moment intimacy means you live in constant connection to Him and you have access to the knowledge that you're deeply loved and specifically purposed.

This isn't a practice to visit in the morning or before you go to sleep. It's like breathing: "*He is with me. I am with Him. I know He is near. I have all I need.*" Like John, you'll learn to love Him in a deep way and you'll get in on more than others simply because you're closer. But how is it possible if you, unlike John, don't get to see Jesus physically in front of you? With so many things that occupy your heart and mind, how do you keep yourself connected to Him? It's possible, and the following are six ways to begin.

1. Believe He exists.

The first step to relating to anyone is to believe that they are there. As babies approach eight months old, they develop something called "object permanence," which is the understanding that people or other objects continue to exist even when they cannot be seen, heard, or otherwise sensed. Until this develops, playing "hide and go seek" with a child is not very fun because the second you hide or are out of sight, they forget you're there.

Our first step in learning to live in a moment-to-moment relationship with God is to believe and know in our hearts that He really is there and to live that way constantly. "And without faith it is impossible to please God, because anyone who comes to him must believe that he exists and that he rewards those who earnestly seek him" (Hebrews 11:6).

This isn't simply mental assent, agreeing that God is there because someone convinced you of the reality. It's just like meeting another individual. Once you meet a person, you know from then on that they exist, and you decide how often you'll relate to them and at what level. It would be strange to meet someone and deny that they exist. With God, your first step to living closely to Him is to believe that He is real—and a rewarder of those who diligently seek Him (See Hebrews 11:6).

2. Invite Jesus into your heart and make the decision to follow Him.

In Luke 5:1-11, we read the extraordinary story of Jesus calling Peter into a deeper relationship with Him.

> One day as Jesus was standing by the Lake of Gennesaret, the people were crowding around him and listening to the word of God. He saw at the water's edge two boats, left there by the fishermen, who were washing their nets. He

got into one of the boats, the one belonging to Simon, and asked him to put out a little from shore. Then he sat down and taught the people from the boat. When he had finished speaking, he said to Simon, "Put out into deep water, and let down the nets for a catch." Simon answered, "Master, we've worked hard all night and haven't caught anything. But because you say so, I will let down the nets." When they had done so, they caught such a large number of fish that their nets began to break. So they signaled their partners in the other boat to come and help them, and they came and filled both boats so full that they began to sink. When Simon Peter saw this, he fell at Jesus' knees and said, "Go away from me, Lord; I am a sinful man!" For he and all his companions were astonished at the catch of fish they had taken, and so were James and John, the sons of Zebedee, Simon's partners. Then Jesus said to Simon, "Don't be afraid; from now on you will fish for people." So they pulled their boats up on shore, left everything and followed him.

Prior to this, Andrew, Peter's brother, had already introduced him to Jesus, and he had been interested in what He had to say. However, in this moment, Jesus turned His attention to Peter to call him into a personal, intimate relationship. Jesus walked into the young man's everyday life and showed Peter who He really was. At the beginning of the story, Peter was a tired, dejected fisherman who had had a really bad day at work, catching no fish all night and trying to clean up his nets and go home. Jesus interrupted his cleaning to ask him for help and then performed a miracle aimed specifically at demonstrating to Peter that He had the power to fulfill the desires of his heart. He showed him that He is more than just a "teacher." He is the Lord of all creation who can fill a net with fish.

Somehow in the middle of the exchange, Peter's heart was confronted not only by Jesus' existence but also by the realization that He is the One his heart had been waiting for his entire life. Peter was left with no choice but to fall down before Jesus and be honest about his heart. Jesus responded to Peter's visceral expression of faith and fear of the Lord, mercifully saying, "Don't worry about the state of your heart, Peter. I can help you. In fact, if you'll open your heart to following me into every part of your life, together we will 'catch' (or reach) and help many others."

There is no way for me or you to develop a life of moment-to-moment intimacy without making the same decision Peter made: *If you believe He is real, will you open your heart to Him? Will you choose to give Him your life? Will you choose to follow Him? Will you let Him replace your broken heart with a heart made alive to love Him?*

3. Sense His presence for the first time and then more regularly.

For most of us, we've already sensed His presence (even if we couldn't identify what it was at the time). This is where we began on the first page of this book. You might have sensed Him in the late hours of the night when you were breaking down in tears, not knowing why, longing for something you can't explain.

You might have sensed Him when listening to a song that somehow hit your heart and filled your eyes with tears. Or maybe it happened when you've watched a beautiful family together, read something that inspired you, or even looked across a starry night or a beautiful sunrise. If you're like most people reading this book, you've sensed "something." The next step for you is to realize that what you felt was Jesus, and then open yourself to sense His presence with you, acknowledging that it's Him.

God is everywhere and in everything. By just stopping or quieting down your thought life and turning off everything else, you can choose or make room for His presence to come into your heart. This ability to sense that He's with you may come and go. Sometimes it may be stronger and other times almost impossible to detect. In truth, He's present with you whether you "feel" it or not. You don't always "feel up to it" when we go to spend time with your friends but the relationships still require an investment of effort in order for it to grow. Learning to know and acknowledge His presence with you takes time and cultivation, especially when it goes directly against how you feel in that instance. Choosing to create space to respond to His presence, regardless of your perception of it, is a key spiritual discipline that you'll need to develop.

4. Set aside part of each day to spend time alone with God.

We live our lives in a world that does not believe in God and actually ridicules those who do. Our lives are busy and constantly filled with things vying for our attention. We also face the realities and responsibilities of our lives that quickly pull us into "fight or flight" tendencies. It can be very easy in the beginning to go five minutes away from your house and to forget that God exists. At the end of a crazy day, you then realize, "Oh man! I forgot You, Jesus. I faced an entire day alone, without you, just the way I did before you came into my life!" Of course, this means that you went an entire day without hearing Him speak.

One way to help you avoid forgetting Jesus is to start your day with a quiet time. This is time that's set apart for you to be quiet, to listen, to read Scripture, and to tell Him that you give Him this day and want to follow Him into it. You can ask Him to teach you to grow closer to Him through every event that you face. You can even talk with Him in tomorrow's quiet time about how you did at staying connected to Him the day before.

Quiet times are a helpful tool to intentionally make room in your heart and mind for your new relationship with Jesus. These quiet times can be rough at first as you feel the unbearable weight of the quiet and struggle not to be distracted. Gradually, however, these times become richer and more vital. They become like going on a "date" with Jesus and they can do a great deal to help you grow closer to Him. At the beginning, this time may even seem like time wasted, but as your faith grows, quiet times will become powerful encounters with Jesus that launch you into staying connected to Him throughout your day.

5. Displace your thoughts for His presence.

The Practice of the Presence of God is a book of collected teachings from a man named Brother Lawrence, a 17th-century Carmelite friar, that chronicles a humble cook's efforts to stay open and connected to God's presence throughout his everyday tasks.[5] In his book, Brother Lawrence focused on continually turning to Jesus in the midst of his day to talk with Him and to stay aware of Jesus being with him. He made it his aim not to "quit His conversation to think of trifles and fooleries."

This sounds simple but, in actually trying to live it out, you will quickly realize that it requires all the effort and discipline of an Olympic athlete. You'll have to make some significant changes to the way you live your life in order to keep your mind focused or even aware of God being close. Most people's thought lives are out of control. When you try to quiet your mind, you are quickly assaulted by worry and fear, and your imagination conjures up all kinds of scenarios that will distract or discourage you.

Faith gives your heart the ability to sense and know an invisible God. This process of learning to live in moment-to-moment intimacy with God is difficult in the beginning when your faith muscles are weak and your thought life is quite strong. With each choice to open your life to Jesus, however, He will do something to show you that He's with you— and that He's amazing. Over time, your faith will grow stronger.

6. Stay in the river of His life.

The God you're working to stay close to is ever present. He's constantly with you and available to you. As you learn to "practice His presence" or to "abide in Him," allowing your heart to live in moment-to-moment connection with Him, you realize you see things incorrectly. Your battle isn't to get closer to Him but to remove all the other things that your heart has grabbed hold of to take His place. In times when the limits of your faith can't see Him, you accept lesser, worthless options. As you find success in quieting our minds and pulling away distractions and substitutes, you fill your heart with Jesus. You learn how to surrender to His love, guidance, and presence.

Like a swimmer resting in the flow of a river, your work becomes less about trying to think about Him and more about staying in the flow of His love, training yourself from thinking about anything else. Each time your heart connects with Jesus, you experience a supernatural peace and sweetness that allows us to "taste and see that the Lord is good" (Psalm 34:8). Your heart and life are trained by this peace to look for Him quickly and constantly and, once you've found Him, to do everything you can to stay close.

From the place of connectedness with the Lord, you hear His voice more clearly and constantly, and your life becomes a continual adventure lived alongside Him—learning His ways and experiencing His love. Living in moment-to-moment intimacy with the Lord sets the stage for you to grow into a life that God will use in powerful ways to impact the lives of others while leading you deeper and deeper into a meaningful relationship with Him, exceeding your dreams of anything you thought possible.

The closer you come to Him, the more you will understand how intimately He loves you, knows you, and helps you, and you'll discover more ways to grow closer and closer. You'll have your own specific ways you draw near to Him. In addition to these six steps, you'll learn what helps you and what doesn't. If you can learn to live your life in moment-to-moment intimacy with Him, every other **forgotten piece** becomes infinitely more accessible. Your faith will rise. Your life will change. And you'll get in on adventures and purpose with Him that were never possible before.

CHAPTER 10

LIVING IN MOMENT-TO-MOMENT INTIMACY WITH GOD: A SUMMARY

The Apostle John was Jesus' closest disciple, and it happened because he chose Jesus every chance he could. He yearned to be close to Him. He didn't forget Jesus for a moment. He loved Him and stayed with Him, even when it was hard to do so.

It's the same when you live in moment-to-moment intimacy with God. You can't love God when you forget about Him. When you're intimately connected, you're consumed by Him. You're constantly aware He's with you, and you long to be closer and closer.

Living in moment-to-moment intimacy with God will fill

you with an assurance that you're okay, no matter the circumstances, because He's with you. This forgotten piece has been left behind because of the numerous other voices vying for your attention and heart. Don't give yourself to them. His is the only presence that will help, heal, and lead you into an abundant life.

In this section, we explored living in moment-to-moment intimacy with God through stories, reasons why it's important to do so, and steps to learn how to live your life this way. As you go deeper into intimacy with God, you will only uncover more of Him. You'll only love Him more and thus receive more from Him. And you'll be different because of the time you spend with Him.

Why learn to live in moment-to-moment intimacy with God?

1. You can hear God's voice continuously.

2. It's easier to obey when you do hear God speak.

3. You displace negative thoughts with joy.

4. You will flourish, grow, and bear effective fruit.

5. You become a person of His presence.

How do you learn to live in moment-to-moment intimacy with God?

1. Believe He exists.

2. Invite Jesus into your heart and make the decision to follow Him.

3. "Sense" His presence for the first time and then do the same more regularly.

4. Set aside part of each day to spend time alone with God.

5. Displace your thoughts for His presence.

6. Stay in the river of His life.

The closer you draw to your Father, the more your sin and hurt will be brought to the surface. Don't let this deter you. This forgotten piece is critical and will lead you into a way of life that keeps you from the chaos and unhelpful patterns of the world. Life in moment-to-moment intimacy with Him is full of His peace, power, help, and purpose. You don't miss out on Him because you don't leave Him and He certainly will never leave you. It's a fuller and better way, and a way you'll need to learn to live a life of consequential faith.

Forgotten Piece Three

EMBRACING A LIFE OF FAITH AND PAIN

"We are hard pressed on every side,
but not crushed;
perplexed, but not in despair;
persecuted, but not abandoned;
struck down, but not destroyed.
We always carry around in our body the
death of Jesus, so that the life of Jesus
may also be revealed in our body"
(2 Corinthians 4:8-10).

CHAPTER 11

JESUS AND PAUL: SUFFERING SERVANTS

If you were trying to decide on two "poster boys" who would influence people to become Christians, you would almost certainly think of Jesus and Paul.

Jesus, the "perfecter of our faith," the one who came to show us what life could be, the one who suffered for every single one of our iniquities, is an obvious first thought.

Jesus' coming to Earth, His miracle-filled, three-year ministry, death on a cross, and resurrection three days later to set us free from our sin are so important that the story is told in its entirety four times in the Bible. These accounts are the gospels of Matthew, Mark, Luke, and John. Every book of the Bible that comes before and every book that comes after points to Jesus.

And then there's Paul, someone with whom we can more readily identify—a selfish man, set on his own path, interrupted, blinded, and turned around for the Kingdom. Paul's ministry impacted the entire world and set a foundation for the modern Christian church, while he also authored much of the New Testament as he lived out his faith—seized by God and His plan.

After Jesus' ascension into heaven, the book of Acts goes on to tell the story of Paul's transformation from murdering Christians to expanding the Kingdom. We read how Paul and his small missionary team spread Christianity as they traveled across the Roman Empire, performing miracles and establishing churches. Most of the books that follow Acts in the Bible are Paul's "epistles," or letters written to young churches to help them grow.

Many consider these two men the most impactful in all of history. These two individuals are great lights whose lives are set before us like the celebrities we put on the covers of cereal boxes to entice people to buy them. Jesus' and Paul's stories inspire us to live out this same supernatural faith that so defined them. We want to be like them.

Jesus

And yet, as we look at these two, as significant and high-impact as they were, the words throughout the pages of the Bible to describe them and what they faced are heavy, intense, and filled with suffering. Jesus was foretold as the Messiah who would be "stricken, oppressed, afflicted, judged, betrayed, accused, and insulted," to list only a few of His descriptors (see Isaiah 53). As for Paul, his list is a famous one: "pressed but not crushed, persecuted, not abandoned, struck down but not destroyed" (2 Corinthians 4). Paul was misunderstood, accused of heresy and put on trial, threatened, sent away, imprisoned, shipwrecked, snake bit, killed (resurrected), and finally martyred.

If these two men are Christianity's biggest advertisements or examples, who in the world would consider buying it? If a life of faith means a life full of pain, suffering, and misunderstanding, who would choose that at all?

There's a secret element at play here, an invisible force, that's stronger than the suffering and deeper than affliction. For Jesus and Paul, their hope anchored in God's abundant, sufficient, and lavish character and provision enables them to transcend the momentary pains that the world inflicts.

For Jesus, the unbearable part of the cross was not being pierced, beaten, and torn apart, it was being separated from the Father, which compelled Him to plead for a different cup (see Matthew 26:39).

Paul was so fully apprehended by this God who set him apart for the purpose of the gospel that he was continually being arrested, smuggled out of cities, and returning to encourage his beloved churches.

While no one wants to choose it, all of us will and do suffer. What draws us to Jesus and to Paul isn't the pain they went through but that somehow their lives transcended human suffering to embody and demonstrate supernatural peace, love, joy, and transformation.

In our world today, too often the Christianity being offered is one that's built around goose-bumps, beautiful music, perfect lighting, and inspirational words. Yet Jesus and Paul show us that this offering isn't Christian at all. It's much closer to the pursuit of "nirvana" in Hinduism, which is defined as "a blissful place or state of oblivion to care or pain."

Often, our choices are driven by fear and motivated by the avoidance of pain. Living this way makes us small and forces us into being selfish, self-centered, and shackled with self-protection and the pursuit of self-interest.

Hope is an alternative way, and it was a driving force for our two heroes.

We can often misunderstand hope. We "hope" things will be different one day. We "hope" that we'll change. But hope isn't a vague thought, and it isn't a form of wishing. Hope is an anchor that holds us fast to a promise we have yet to see fulfilled. Hope is substance when our own self and being lack strength. Hope is the ability to endure difficulty for the days, weeks, years, decades it takes to see the completion of a dream, a calling, a purpose.

We don't suffer well because we do not hope well. Our faith wavers, because faith itself is the substance of things *hoped* for.

Jesus left Heaven to come down and suffer as we do; the Bible says He was tempted in every way as we are (See Hebrews 4:15). Isaiah says there was nothing attractive about Him, nothing to draw us to Him (See Isaiah 53:1). He was tempted by the enemy. He was mocked and discredited by the leadership of His day. He had to endure the disciples in their messiness and disobedience. He was denied by

His family and eventually by most of His closest followers. And of course, on the cross, He endured the suffering we all deserved because of our sin.

But Jesus wasn't downcast. To be near Him was to have access to God in a way never before possible. A touch of His robe took away sickness. Jesus was joyful; He had a sense of humor. Though the greatest suffering there ever will be was put upon Him, His story is defined by humility, by closeness to His Father, by being provided for and completely loved, by total commitment to His mission.

Paul

Paul wasn't circumstantially much better. Paul begins his walk with God by being rejected by the disciples, who couldn't believe that their former persecutor had been transformed for the Kingdom. Wherever Paul went, there were plots to kill him, and in one instance, they did. Paul was stoned to death, his body dragged out of the city, and when he was resurrected, he went back (see Acts 14:19-20).

And yet Paul wrote repeatedly in his letters about hope. He encouraged churches in their walk with the Lord, and he didn't consider his own life of any value to himself—he was determined to complete the ministry set before him by Jesus. He was an instrument for the Lord, specifically set apart for a unique mission to the Gentiles.

Embracing a life of faith and pain can't be at all about the pain. We already suffered without the Lord and His transformation, due to the sin of our wrecked, messy hearts. In the Lord, we still suffer. We are, after all, called to take up our cross, deny ourselves, and follow Him. We will be misunderstood and rejected by the world around us. The Lord will lead us into the hardest places, the darkest places.

But we don't follow Him in order to suffer; we follow Him because there's life, abundant life, that is bigger and beyond suffering. It offers us things that suffering can't touch or take away.

And as you're faithful to follow even when it hurts, His Holy Spirit will build faith in you and a hope that simply will not let go even in the face of the whole world shaking. Your motivators will change; no longer will you consider suffering the cost. You will see it as an opportunity to go deeper into His comfort and love to keep you regardless of the obstacle. The suffering will seem almost unnoticeable when you're closest to Him. You'll see it all as "great gain," getting to be with the Lord in His redemptive work for your life and the lives of others.

Growing in this hope, this ability to hang on to our faith, to what God has said to us, even in the face of the greatest difficulties, makes our lives like Jesus' and Paul's. We find a place of intimate fellowship with God that meets us, comforts us and sustains us in the flames of adversity. We become overcomers, living lives marked by the patience, endurance, and power that changes people's lives on the way to transforming the world.

This forgotten piece is mind boggling and counter-intuitive at the same time. Most people come to faith because they're tired, worn out, and broken from the pain of their own choices and sin. Why would anyone then embrace a life of faith *and* pain? Though it may be easier to imagine why this piece is often forgotten, it's important that we know why it matters. Following Jesus means following Him into His ways of life, and we'll be required to follow Him into things that go against what is natural to us and what makes sense in the world. Remember, He'll give you hope and help as you go with Him and know that being with Him, even when there's suffering, is far more worthwhile than any comfort you can find on your own. In the following chapters, you will read more stories and receive practical help so you can dive deeper into why this piece is critical for your life.

CHAPTER 12

A GLIMPSE OF EMBRACING A LIFE OF FAITH AND PAIN

I first saw Kathy in a crowded tourist mall. We both worked at stores across the hallway from each other. I fell in love with her instantly. She was beautiful—the princess I had been searching for my entire life. By the end of that night, we had the names of our future children written down on a napkin. A year later, almost to the day, we were married.

After growing up in difficult and painful situations, Kathy and I did everything we could to make sure our relationship was in God's will. We were both new followers of Jesus. We stayed close to the couple discipling us and worked hard in our roles as youth pastors at our church. We prayed every day that God would lift us out of our difficult pasts to build a strong marriage.

Ten months later, I was crying on my living room floor. Kathy had left. The pain was overwhelming. Night after night, I screamed myself to sleep. The enemy Jesus had so clearly defeated had reached into our lives and taken my wife. For the first time in my life, following Jesus was not beautiful. It was horrific.

At work one day, I cried out to God: "Why would You do this to me? I love You and You brought Kathy into my life. We prayed and asked You and You showed us it was Your will for us to be together. Why would You let this happen? How could You let her be lost?" The Lord answered with a strength and hope that surprised me almost as much as His words did: "You don't want to do that. You don't want to begin asking why right now. If you start questioning why I'm doing this thing, you'll have to question everything I've done for you: saving you, bringing you home to me—all of it."

In the next year, I moved to a different city to be in a community where I could receive the support I needed. People in my church held me as I cried. They prayed for me, fed me dinner, and invited me into their families. The desperation of the situation drew me closer and closer to God and into a level of dependence I had never before experienced. Because of my brokenness and the moment-to-moment need I had for Jesus to be everything to me just to make it through the day, my dependence spilled over to everyone around me. Miraculous stories began to happen. People began meeting Jesus as I saw the power of God in ways that I had before only read about. Yet still, Kathy was gone.

One day, pulling out of a Taco Bell drive-through, I heard the Lord say, "You don't trust me." I quickly responded, while wolfing down a soft taco, that of course I did. But He repeated: "You don't trust me." After going back and forth with Him for a few minutes, my voice cracked and tears began streaming down my face and I said, "How can I trust you? You just gave me the most beautiful gift and then made me watch her go away and be destroyed. How could I trust you?" The Lord answered, almost playfully, "Great. Now you are relating to me honestly."

Within a few months, my phone rang. It was Kathy. She wanted to know if she could come home. She wanted to know if I could ever love her again. I told her I had never stopped. Our journey from there wasn't an easy one, but we had learned a secret: God is loving and powerful. He protects us from the enemy but He's building our hearts to be able to follow Him even "as we walk through the valley of the shadow of death." Learning to follow Him, even when it hurts, has led us closer to Him and deeper into His purposes.

CHAPTER 13

WHY EMBRACE A LIFE OF FAITH AND PAIN?

You are called to follow Jesus, and following Him means going with Him into His purpose and in the way He directs. His way wasn't the most popular or easy one; many turned away, denied Him, or crucified Jesus because they couldn't or didn't want to believe Him and what He said. Jesus and those who follow Him are called to a life of bringing God's Kingdom of light into a dark, hurting world. It is never an easy displacement; the sin and hurt in you and others will do their best to hold on and fight back (this is the reason for pain and suffering).

But Jesus has overcome it all, and He'll give you every bit of the faith, hope, and help you need to stand in the midst of the battles, see His bigger purposes at work, and not be damaged in the midst of the difficulty and pain. If you give up when there's pain, you'll miss out on some of the best parts of being with Him—learning to transcend suffering, taking part in the victory of good over evil in the lives of others, and getting to be with Him every moment in every way. The following are six specific reasons why it's important to embrace a life of faith and pain.

1. Your faith deepens.

For many of us, the word "faith" seems to describe some mysterious substance we know we need but don't understand. The Bible uses men and women throughout the Old and New testaments to show us that faith is actually just hearing what God says to us (or receiving His direction) and honoring the Lord by responding to Him. He told Abraham to go and Abraham went (see Genesis 12). He sent Moses on a mission and Moses, albeit reluctantly, accepted it (see Exodus 3-12). Jesus only did what the Father told Him to do and only said what the Father told Him to say (see John 5:19). Jesus called Peter to walk onto the water, and Peter responded (see Matthew 14:22-29). This is faith.

While it takes faith to hear and respond to anything an invisible God says to you, some words from God require more faith than others. Smaller decisions and steps of obedience that correspond to your current life situations and culture require less faith than when God asks you to do something that seems impossible. Abraham faced what the Danish philosopher, Søren Kierkegaard calls, "the dark night of the soul," when God asked him to take his son—the son he had been promised by the Lord—and hike up a hill and sacrifice him to God (see Genesis 22:1-19).

Kierekegaard calls this "the teleological suspension of the ethical"—when God asks you to do something that seems wrong.[6] The story ends with God providing Abraham with a ram in a thicket to sacrifice instead of his son, but Abraham demonstrated a deep faith in God's goodness not to have turned back in horror on the way up the mountain.

Living a life of faith requires you to live, not by the outward appearance, but by *"every word that proceeds from the mouth of God"* (Deuteronomy 8:3). You learn, as a spiritual athlete, how to trust God and follow Him even when it appears that doing so is impossible or will cost you everything. God doesn't say outlandish things to provoke you or to be cruel but to train you to grow in your trust of His goodness, His faithfulness, and His ways. This may bring suffering but it will lead you into a life that is no longer limited by circumstances, emotion, or disappointments, and deepen your once-weak faith. By living in faith you are free to obey and walk with the God who created our universe by His voice.

2. You are set free from the jail cell of yourself.

Each of us in a personal desert of disconnection from God bound by selfishness, self-seeking, and self-centeredness that makes our lives narrow and dead. Jesus walks into your lifeless world and demonstrates to you an unselfish love that continually seeks the good of others. As you follow God's voice and presence into "living a life of love" (Ephesians 5:1), the first captive set free is you. Peter wrote, "Therefore, since Christ suffered in his body, arm yourselves also with the same attitude, because whoever suffers in the body is done with sin" (1 Peter 4:1). Suffering is an actual invitation to escape a defensive, self-consumed survival mode of living and to instead live a life that is free to love, share, and help others. Suffering retrains you to see that the constant pursuit of what feels good or looks good often keeps you from many of the things in life that are truly good.

3. Your life is filled with His love, and you're comforted in the midst of suffering.

"For just as we share abundantly in the sufferings of Christ, so also our comfort abounds through Christ" (2 Corinthians 1:5). Our deep desire is to be loved. After looking for love in all of the wrong places, in Jesus we, at last, find the thing we have been searching for: comfort. Our hearts were originally designed to be constant conduits of God's voice. We were made to walk closely with Him, hearing and responding to His voice and speaking back to Him. We were made for an intimate relationship built around conversation and interaction. This is the "image of God," the actual way that Father, Son and Holy Spirit relate to one another and it is what we were made for.

Losing this in the Garden was like a desert adventurer losing their supply of water. Every day without communion with God scorches your heart like the searing heat of the sun and the dry, oven blast of the hot wind. As you open your heart to Jesus, the fount of love you once lost comes rushing in, and you experience refreshment, relief, and salvation. This is what it is to receive comfort from God. Jesus touches you with the "river whose streams make glad" your heart and mind (see Psalm 46:4), and you are flooded with peace, rest, satisfaction, contentment, and security.

After being in a cool place drinking as much water as they could want, a person has far greater capacity to head back into the heat of the desert to rescue another. Having now received comfort from God, with your heart overflowing in the peace of being right with Him, you experience compassion for others who have not yet experienced the same sweetness. You even find that as you go to comfort the brokenhearted and see hurting people find help, the Holy Spirit goes with you, and you are refreshed along the way.

This is a powerful secret: what for others would be terrible suffering, is different for us. Miraculously, even as we face rejection, attack, abuse, being misunderstood and persecuted by people as we lay our lives down to love them, the Holy Spirit continues to give us comfort and peace. The more we are maligned and mishandled by people, the deeper we experience God's love: "Praise be to the God and Father of our Lord Jesus Christ, the Father of compassion and the God of all comfort, who comforts us in all our troubles, so that we can comfort those in any trouble with the comfort we ourselves receive from God" (2 Corinthians 1:4-5).

4. You get to know Jesus and His power and thus will become like Him in transcending the suffering of this world.

"I want to know Christ—yes, to know the power of his resurrection and participation in his sufferings, becoming like him in his death" (Philippians 3:10). Many times today, even in churches, we can fall into a trap of believing that the experience of God's presence is only found in the emotional experiences of beautiful music performed by beautiful people in beautiful auditoriums with beautiful ambience. Doing so raises up the next generation of young leaders who believe that the things of God will always and only feel good, sound good, and look good, judging from the outward appearance. This trains these leaders in a way that misses out on so much of who Jesus really is as the "suffering servant."

Jesus often went the opposite direction than the crowd. He often said things that were either hard for people without faith to grasp or that were an outright offense to His listeners. Many times today, we watch the world at large reject religion and Jesus, not because they're not drawn to Jesus, but because they see nothing special or real in those who represent Christianity. Their hearts are open, longing for Him, but they see little connection between the superficiality of so-called "Christians" and the One who is drawing their hearts.

Suffering is a pathway that leads you out and away from culture and popular religion and leads you to know Jesus. He's not the pre-packaged, Hollywood version of a savior that many present but is more like the lion Aslan in C.S. Lewis' Narnia series who isn't safe but he is good (*The Chronicles of Narnia*).[7] When you begin to hear His voice, His thoughts, and His will to experience His presence and to be led by His Spirit, you are in touch with the power that raised Jesus from the grave 2,000 years ago. This power begins to flow through your life, and you see miracles and people's lives begin to be changed just as your life has been changed.

When you fall so in love with Him that staying close to Him is your deepest desire, you find yourself going with Him into uncomfortable circumstances that include loss, rejection, and worse. Yet you hardly notice that these things are happening because your eyes are fixed on Him and you are enjoying His company, His words, and His life. As this deeper and deeper experience of communion with Him and comfort from Him occurs, your life becomes like His, transcending suffering rather than avoiding it.

5. You grow in hope.

Faith comes when God speaks to us and leads us to action. When God speaks and we believe what He says, that is called faith. However, when God has spoken and everything around us doesn't immediately demonstrate God's promises or words, we call this "hope." Hebrews 11 tells us that "faith is the substance of things hoped for, the evidence of things not seen" (Hebrews 11:1). Hope takes the substance of what we have heard and holds onto it, enabling us to suffer through waiting for what we believe will come but cannot see. Many of the people we read about in Scripture died before some things that God had said to them came about. This can sound sad but it's actually a way of living that allows for great things to be accomplished.

When you first come to faith, you feel a little bit crazy responding to something that no one around you believes and to someone that few people close to you can experience or hear. You step out a bit and worry when you don't immediately receive evidence that what you believe is real. You're like the disciple Thomas, who asks to put his hands in Jesus' wounds to know that it is really Him. Jesus lets Thomas do so but says to him, "Because you have seen me, you have believed; blessed are those who have not seen and yet have believed" (John 20:29). To not see and yet believe is what we call hope, and it leads to qualities in a person that empower them to accomplish great things.

Romans 5:3-5 says, "Not only so, but we also glory in our sufferings, because we know that suffering produces perseverance; perseverance, character; and character, hope, and hope does not disappoint." Hope is tied to character, which is the ability to do what is right even when it hurts. This character produces perseverance, the ability to suffer for long periods of time without stopping. Perseverance gives you a long list of capacities like patience, endurance, and other things that allow you to be kind, to love well and to help others, even and especially when it hurts. Suffering is both the school that develops hope which allows you to endure, opening your life more deeply to a life like Jesus and to partnering with Him so you can impact the lives of others.

6. You learn to live a life of love that helps others.

Suffering shapes the one who suffers, and it's also a powerful tool for reaching and impacting them. Paul writes in Romans 2:4 that, "God's kindness is intended to lead you to repentance." The Greek word for *kindness* is *chrestotes*, which is defined as "meeting real needs, in God's way, in

His timing."[8] When Jesus did miracles during His three-year ministry, He did so out of *chrestotes* or *kindness*, demonstrating to others that the Kingdom of God was the answer to the problems they faced which included accessing His power that could help them.

When Jesus helped a blind person see (see Mark 8:22-26) or a lame person walk (see Matthew 9:1-8) or when He turned to an adulterous woman and told her she was forgiven (see John 8:1-11), He was entering people's lives and taking away the toxic burdens that were destroying them. These kindnesses were such significant demonstrations of God's love and power that people most often believed in and then followed Him. He used these helpful miracles to show them He was what they needed.

This way of walking into other's lives to help them required Jesus to consider others before Himself. As such, a basic definition of ministry is to devote your life to meeting others' needs over our own. When you begin to live by faith, Jesus invites you to become one with His heart for people. You sense His heart for hurting people around you: the teller at the bank, the cashier at the grocery store, a family member at your table, or a coworker in your office. As you pay attention to what He is impressing upon your heart, you begin to respond. You begin a conversation and watch as the Holy Spirit opens a space for you to demonstrate care, and to listen, help, and pray with and for them that God will help them.

At times, God moves in their lives in a visible way, helping them immediately. More often, however, God requires you to move slower, building a connection and then a friendship that earns their trust and further down the road impacts them. This work of following Jesus into caring for others requires that you lay down your own pursuits so you can enter into the concerns of someone else, and this is a form of suffering in itself. You end up denying yourself to follow His lead into another person's life. Without the capacity to live by faith and to embrace pain or discomfort, you would not have the ability to participate with Jesus in this part of the "fellowship of His sufferings" and, as a result, you would miss out on witnessing "the power of His resurrection" (Philippians 3:10) as He powerfully touches their lives.

Over time, Jesus will train you to pursue these opportunities more diligently so you can love others sacrificially. Your concern for hurting people may at times find them lashing out, attacking, or misunderstanding you. Your commitment to Jesus to care for a person who has not yet found faith will often be misperceived and leave them suspicious of your motives, or even your sanity. When you sense God's love for someone and choose to love them even when it exposes you to ill treatment, it becomes possible for people to see that it is God's *agape* love that is motivating you.

Every other kind of love you experience, including romantic love, friendship, and familial connections repays us with some amount of reciprocity. We love because we are loved. Agape love is different in that it requires nothing in return. The love we see in John 3:16, "For God so loved the world that He gave His only begotten Son that whoever believes in Him shall not perish but have eternal life" is agape love. Even when loving us meant Jesus was rejected, accused, condemned, and crucified, He continued loving us. *Agape* love is sacrificial and because of that, it's capable of reaching and loving those no one else could. When we learn to follow Jesus in faith into loving people who do not love us back, we are given a powerful opportunity to demonstrate to them this supernatural, God-given, God-powered *agape* love, and they are impacted by its power.

It's not possible to live a life without pain. You'll either endure the pain of your sin on your own, attempting constantly to sedate or distract yourself from the hurt, or you'll participate in a productive pain. This isn't pain for the sake of pain, but pain for the sake of learning to endure, building faith, waiting on Him, and seeing your life and the lives of others transformed for good. The verse from Philippians 3:10 is a perfect summary of the purpose for learning to live a life of faith even when there is pain: "I want to know Christ—yes, to know the power of his resurrection and participation in his sufferings, becoming like him in his death."

The question is not whether you'll suffer, but whether you'll suffer for righteousness, peace, joy, and the other promises of the Lord. Will you learn to follow Him, even when it's uncomfortable, costly, ugly, and misunderstood? When you do, you'll "become like Him," get to be with Him, see people freed from lies and hurt, and you'll then uncover the unmatchable power of following Jesus into the life you were made to live.

CHAPTER 14

HOW TO EMBRACE A LIFE OF FAITH AND PAIN

There's no way to embrace a life of faith and pain without a significant and substantive relationship with Jesus—nor is there any reason to do so. Embracing a life of faith even when there's suffering is only made possible when you stay close enough to God to hear Him tell you where you're supposed to go and to receive everything you'll need from Him to stand in the midst of difficult, painful things. This forgotten piece isn't possible to achieve without hearing and obeying His voice and living in moment-to-moment intimacy with God. You'll need the closeness and direction in order to absolutely know you're where you need to be and you're enduring what you need to endure. Each piece is critical to the other, and you'll see how they build one upon the other. This third piece is no exception. The following are five ways you can learn to embrace a life of faith even when there's pain.

1. Take up your cross, deny yourself, and follow Him.

Jesus teaches His disciples that there's no other way to

God, to fullness of life, and to miraculous power without following Him. In His first moments with the disciples, Jesus calls them by commanding that they follow Him. And He says it again and again to us: We have to follow Him. We follow Him in His ways to seek first the Kingdom of God. We follow Him in His ministry to others through God's ministry first to us. And most importantly, we follow Him to the cross, where we lay down our lives. We die to ourselves, and we are resurrected with Him into new life.

This is perhaps the wildest and most difficult part of Jesus' commands and ways. But there's no way to the things you need and want, like His care, provision, miracles without first encountering the cross. While it's certainly more convenient and less painful when you don't share in this kind of suffering, you don't get to live full lives of faith without this part: taking up your cross of denying your old self and all its ways in order to follow Him. You don't get to take anything of the dead ways with you on this journey—even the ones you like, are comforted by, or "aren't that bad."

As extreme as it sounds and as dramatic as it may feel, the amazing thing about a cross experience is that it leads to life. The crucifixion of your old self leads to a deep, powerful access to His Holy Spirit, and the promise that will enable you to transcend suffering and effectively walk in faith. First, the way of the cross, which leads to every part of your being cared for and comforted by God as you walk into the deep, mind-boggling adventures for which you yearn.

2. Listen to what God is saying and do it.

You cannot and should not pursue suffering, for suffering for the sake of suffering is foolish. Your pursuit has to be to hear and respond to God's voice and guidance. When He says go, you go. When He says say something, you speak. Embracing a life of faith and pain means that suffering, ambiguity, discomfort, and even persecution can't be allowed to dissuade or discourage you from continuing to follow Jesus or obeying His voice.

3. When the pain and pressure come, cast your burdens onto Jesus.

Even as you respond to God's voice and suffering comes,

you aren't to suffer in silence or endure it on your own. These moments of suffering require you to turn to God immediately and ask for His help as the Scriptures direct you to do: "Cast your burden upon the Lord and He will sustain you; He will never allow the righteous to be shaken" (Psalm 55:22); "Cast all your cares upon Him, for He cares for you" (1 Peter 5:7); and "Whoever finds their life will lose it, and whoever loses their life for my sake will find it" (Matthew 10:39).

Jesus commanded His followers not to care for themselves because their Father in heaven would care for them (see Matthew 6:26). To "cast your cares" upon God is to go to Him after things happen that cause you anxiety or discomfort, asking Him to help you. He's good and faithful, and He won't leave you alone to face more than you can handle.

4. Receive His care, comfort, and consolation.

In times of suffering in faith, you are to cry out to God and He will provide His help, His *chrestotes*, to you. A cruel Father would send you into an endeavor only to leave you and allow you to be hurt. But our Father is consistently good. While He may use the opportunity to teach you to wait, to be patient, or even to grow deeper in faith, He will be with you to protect and comfort you. Every aspect of your pain will be met by His ministry to you. In fact, to the extent that you suffer, you will receive His consolation.

One of the best ways to experience the deepest expressions of God's love, care, and comfort is to step out with faith into moments that require it. He is faithful and He won't allow you to be separated from His love as Paul reminded us:

> What, then, shall we say in response to these things? If God is for us, who can be against us? He who did not spare his own Son, but gave him up for us all—how will he not also, along with him, graciously give us all things? Who will bring any charge against those whom God has chosen? It is God who justifies. Who then is the one who condemns? No one. Christ Jesus who

died—more than that, who was raised to life—is at the right hand of God and is also interceding for us. Who shall separate us from the love of Christ? Shall trouble or hardship or persecution or famine or nakedness or danger or sword? As it is written: 'For your sake we face death all day long; we are considered as sheep to be slaughtered.' No, in all these things we are more than conquerors through him who loved us. For I am convinced that neither death nor life, neither angels nor demons, neither the present nor the future, nor any powers, neither height nor depth, nor anything else in all creation, will be able to separate us from the love of God that is in Christ Jesus our Lord (Romans 8:31-39).

5. Make it your purpose to love others guided by the Holy Spirit.

As you receive more and more of God's comfort and love, you will have more and more to share with the hurting people around you. Your heart will become more like His heart for hurting people. Your life's purpose is then to go through each day looking for the opportunities to hear His voice and care for the people in your world. Former Wycliffe Bible translator, Dr. Dow Robinson, said, "You have no idea how much trouble God goes through to decide who your neighbors are going to be!" God is sovereign and sets the people around you each day that He will care for through you: "You are God's dear children, so try to be like him. Live a life of love. Love others just as Christ loved us. He gave himself for us—a sweet-smelling offering and sacrifice to God" (Ephesians 5:1-2).

This **forgotten piece** can feel like a well-kept secret; you certainly won't hear about it in the mainstream way of living. While many around you will work to build a life of comforts and consolations, you'll be freed to live a life that isn't defined by the avoidance of difficult, painful things. Instead, you'll have access to faith that enables you to transcend suffering, endure hardship, and step out into significant impact on your friends, family, neighbors, coworkers, and passersby. Jesus' life wasn't defined by what He suffered; His life was defined by His amazing, life-altering relationship with the Father that included pain—but also led Him into the most important moments for all of hu-man-kind. May it be so for you, and may He give you great faith for the battle you were created to fight.

A Disclaimer for
Embracing a Life of Faith and Pain

Embracing a life of faith and pain is to step away from a life of consolations and self-consumption in exchange for the pursuit of Jesus' words and ways. As you do this, there will be moments that are uncomfortable, difficult, and painful to your flesh and soul. It's the practice of exchanging that pain for faith in what God is saying. And eventually, you transcend the pain into a life of selfless service.

We encourage you to look to Jesus constantly as your example—a life of only saying and doing what God has said. When Jesus suffered, it was at the leading of the Spirit at the right time for the ultimate purpose of God's great plan of redemption.

This piece neither encourages or condones the pursuit of abusive and dangerous situations where you're being taken advantage of or damaged, nor does it require you to be in a place of enabling the disobedience of others. If you feel you're in a situation where you're being taken advantage of or unsafe at the hands of others, turn to the authorities in your life who you can trust and step away from that situation immediately.

CHAPTER 15

EMBRACING A LIFE OF FAITH AND PAIN: A SUMMARY

Jesus and Paul are our examples in faith. Jesus showed us how to live perfectly connected to the Father. Paul, a messier, sinful example, demonstrates for us how completely the Lord redeems and uses us as broken people to live lives of faith. Both these men changed the world with their lives, and both of their stories are filled with difficult, painful circumstances.

God doesn't promise us a painless life of bliss. Numbed out and kept from pain, we would miss out on an important part of the faith experience. God will lead you into hard and difficult situations, not unlike the ones He saved you from, in order to use you to displace darkness with light. When you follow Him, you'll be set free from the pain of your own brokenness, and you'll be called into a life of helping others experience the same.

This isn't a reason to be anxious or draw back. It's actually a reason to press in, and grow closer to God. You'll be called to embrace a life of faith and pain, and when you do, you'll participate in a kind of faith that enables you to transcend pain, to overcome hurt, and to help set others free.

In this section, we detailed embracing a life of faith and pain including stories from our own lives, reasons why, and ways to live this way.

Why learn to embrace a life of faith and pain?

1. Your faith deepens.
2. You're set free from the jail cell of yourself.
3. Your life is filled with His love, and you're comforted in the midst of suffering.
4. You get to know Jesus and His power and thus will become like Him in transcending the suffering of this world.
5. You grow in hope.
6. You learn to live a life of love that helps others.

How do you embrace a life of faith and pain?

1. Take up your cross, deny yourself, and follow Him.
2. Listen to what God is saying and do it.
3. When the pain and pressure come, cast your burdens onto Jesus.
4. Receive His care, comfort, and consolation.
5. Make it your purpose to love others guided by the Holy Spirit.

This is a counter-intuitive **forgotten piece** for obvious reasons. Pain for the sake of pain is pointless and not what He's calling you to. Pain and momentary afflictions for the sake of His great purposes will be required in living a life of faith. As you recognize this, learn to hear His voice to know you're where He has said to stand and fight, the battles will be different, and the victories much more impactful. You need to remember this forgotten piece because it was the example set before us in Jesus, and it will enable you to transcend suffering so you can see His ways unleashed in your life and the lives of those you know and love.

FINDING AND FULFILLING GOD'S PURPOSE FOR YOUR LIFE

"[God] has saved us and called us with a holy calling, not according to our works, but according to His own purpose and grace, which was given to us in Christ Jesus before time began"
(2 Timothy 1:9).

CHAPTER 16

ABRAHAM: THE PROMISE FOLLOWER

Were you made for something specific? Does your life have a reason for its existence? Is there one thing that you were created to do, to build, to fight for?

The answer to each question is a resounding yes.

God cares specifically and uniquely for each of us. We were knit together in our mother's wombs, and before our lives began, our days were numbered. He laid out every day of our lives, and He knows our choices before we make them. He is purposeful, working *everything* together for the good of those who love Him and according to His eternal counsels laid before the creation of the world. And because we are made in His image, we too are purposed.

So, how do you know? How do you find the one thing you are made for? It seems trite that aptitude tests and personality assessments would capture the work of the Almighty God. (It is.)

And though we have our giftings, specific passions, and desires and interests, God is a relational God. Instead of handing out results on a slip of paper, He's interested in walking out each day of your life with you, making promises, revealing His purpose for your life as faith, hope, and love build up in your heart.

There's no better example of this than Abraham.

Abraham's story begins with God's voice. God told Abraham (Abram at that point) to leave the land where he lived with his family for a place that God *would* show him. There's a recurring pattern in Abraham's journey. God speaks (often big promises), and Abraham responds. And though he hasn't yet seen the fulfillment of the last promise, God makes another promise.

Though Abraham himself struggles and waivers—even to the point of causing harm to others—God persists with Abraham. They talk together. Abraham recognizes his position before God. He obeys; he believes. And his story is amazing.

Abraham's purpose is to have a family—a family that God would create, that God would bless and that would outnumber the stars in the sky.

And though they were old and barren when God sent Abraham and Sarah to an unknown land, God's first promise is four-fold:

1. God will make them a great nation.
2. God will bless those who bless him.
3. He will curse those who dishonor him.
4. And in him, all the families of the Earth shall be blessed.

God doesn't start small; He begins with a massive, exceptional promise. And Abraham went, his whole family and household in tow, unsure of where he would end up.

When they arrive at the land God had directed them to leave everything for, they find it occupied. Still, God promised it to Abraham's descendants, and Abraham believed and worshiped God in that place.

Later they go on to Egypt because there was famine in the land. There, for fear that he would be killed, he was dishonest with Pharaoh claiming that Sarah (his wife) was his sister, and Pharoah took Sarah as his wife. And because it was outside of God's purpose, God cursed the Pharaoh, and he sent Abraham out with an abundance of possessions.

Repeatedly, God afflicted anyone who interferes with the purpose He has for Abraham. He keeps Abraham, protects him, provides for him, and ushers him onward towards the fulfillment of these audacious promises.

Abraham did recognize God as his God, and throughout his whole story, God came to him with different names—names like Lord of Heaven and Earth, Lord Almighty, Everlasting, the Lord Who Will Provide. With each step of Abraham's journey, the Lord revealed more of himself as He revealed more of Abraham's purpose.

And Abraham obeyed. He believed. He went where the Lord told him to go. He related fully to God; they conversed. He recognized the Lord's words as truer than the happenings around him. And in his journey, Abraham surfed his circumstances; He did not let them rule. Though he did not see the fruit of these promises, He believed, and it built in him hope, anchored to the voice of the Lord more than the world around him. It built faith in him to obey the next time and the time after that. It built love for the Lord and His ways. Abraham became a man of God and had hold of the deeper things that are inaccessible by the world.

God went on to promise Abraham that his descendants would be the same as the number of the stars in the heavens. He told him how He would lead his people into the land that was promised, even though Abraham would not see it. He promised Abraham a son born of Sarah in their old age. He promised to spare his nephew Lot. He promised to make a way for all the men in his family to walk cleanly before God. He promised that Abraham would live to a good, old age, and he would die and go to his fathers in peace.

And as specifically as He spoke with Abraham, Abraham responded. He went when the Lord told him. He made sacrifices at the Lord's instruction. He recognized the Lord when He sent visitors to share His promise with Sarah. He honored his father's family. He circumcised every man in his household, including himself and his son, Isaac. He responded to Sarah's voice because the Lord said so, even though it displeased him.

Abraham so believed and feared God that he took the son that is the fulfillment of all these promises, laid him down on the altar, and raised the blade to sacrifice him at the

Lord's direction. Against the reasonable, the circumstantial, the ways of the world, and the natural inclinations of his own flesh, Abraham believed God, and God was faithful to complete every part of the purpose.

Purpose journeys look like that.

The Lord isn't interested in helping you get a hold of what you are made for, if you get there without Him. He hasn't created you for things outside of His ways and rule. He's the God of Heaven and Earth. He is the God Almighty (having complete power). He's everlasting. He's the provider. He is. And your purpose is wrapped up in Him.

To learn and walk out your purpose, you'll need to hear what He says and obey it. You'll need to love Him and know He's with you, because it will not always look or feel like your unique, exceptional purpose is near or even possible. It will hurt; sometimes it will be confusing. But the journey of finding and fulfilling God's purpose for your life is the journey; it's the adventure we get to go on with Him. And it's what makes our life and faith complete.

What will He promise you? What has He purposed for you? Who has He called you to? All these things He'll speak to you. All these things He'll provide for. All these things He'll overcome for. And the fulfillment of the purpose of God in your life will go on to impact others and build the Kingdom and larger purposes of God.

CHAPTER 17

A GLIMPSE OF FINDING AND FULFILLING GOD'S PURPOSE FOR YOUR LIFE

After two years of praying to hear God's voice, on my eighteenth birthday and after a horrible night, I walked into my bedroom, fell to my knees next to my bed, and cried out to Him for help. For the first time in my life, I heard Him speak, saying, "You'll go to Latin America and raise up young leaders." I got up from my knees and typed that line on a typewriter at my desk. He wasn't finished. He continued to speak. I got up and went to my parents and asked them what I should do if the Lord was speaking to me and wouldn't stop. They said, "Go back and listen!"

I had been given one other clue about God's purpose for my life a little more than a year before that incident when a youth pastor agreed to meet with me to help me make a big decision about where to go to college. After hearing my story, he asked me, "Have you ever thought about working with young people?" I asked him if they pay people to do that and he responded, "Not very much."

Prior to this idea of working with young people and God speaking about developing young leaders in Latin America, my family had always teased me that I was a little good at a lot of things but not great at anything. They were specifically worried about my capacity to earn a living. Yet with each glimpse of God's purposes for me, I saw that I was a perfect fit for what He had created me for. I was just funny enough to keep young people's attention, just artistic enough to design the materials needed to mobilize them, and just athletic enough to play the hours of basketball necessary to get to young men's hearts.

The day after my eighteenth birthday, I walked into the history department of my university and changed my major to Latin American history. Within a year, I met my wife—a Costa Rican. Step after step, I watched as my life moved with supernatural force toward this supernatural purpose that God decided before the creation of the Earth that I would accomplish by walking with Him.

Time and time again, I find myself stepping into something that I know is impossible for me but that is tied to His purpose. Knowing this, I step up to the impossibility of it, waiting to see how God will come in and accomplish it. The process hasn't been without tremendous suffering but I can say clearly that knowing He's at work in it to bring me closer and closer to the goal has given me extraordinary peace.

In 2004, my wife and three children and I got on a plane to go to San Jose, Costa Rica, where we lived for six years. Boy With a Ball, the organization we were a part of founding, works now around the world, reaching young people and equipping them to turn and transform their communities. With every hiccup and every roadblock, knowing what God created me for and has called me to do has given me confidence in believing that "He who began a good work in [me] will be faithful to complete it" (see Philippians 1:6). Knowing God's purpose for our lives invites us into a lifetime "date" with God, a journey into His heart and into seeing His power each day.

CHAPTER 18

WHY FIND AND FULFILL GOD'S PURPOSE FOR YOUR LIFE?

Though the third **forgotten piece** might be the one that causes the most pause, this piece is probably part of the reason you went looking for the Lord in the first place. Besides turning to Him to help heal the brokenness in your heart, you probably also have a strong desire to know what in the world He made you for. Why are you here? What is the one wild, important, world-changing thing you are made to do with your life? Though you may have some glimpses or ideas, you'll need the Lord to take you on a purpose journey. You'll need Him to tell you what you were made for, who you were made for, and how you were made to do it.

This purpose He has given you will overwhelm your heart with His care for you, His intentionality with you, and His love for you. You'll learn you were made for greater things than you can imagine. You'll learn that you need Him more than you can think or know. You'll see impossible things.

You'll help people. And this purpose He has given you will change the world. You aren't the only one who needs to find and fulfill your purpose. Your exact purpose is needed by many others who will be reached and redeemed by this part of your relationship with Him. The following chapter contains five reasons why you need to find and fulfill God's purpose for your life.

1. Your life is filled with vision.

Proverbs 29:18 says that "where there is no vision, the people perish." Other versions say that "the people cast off restraint." When an athlete is training to compete in the Olympics, they have a picture in their head of walking into the opening of the games, representing their country. They think of staying in the Olympic Village, of competing, and of standing on the platform to receive a medal. This "vision" of the Olympics fills them with a desire to realize it so strongly that it's an easy choice to say no to anything that will distract them from achieving their goal. This is the power of vision.

The God who created us and who understands us better than we understand ourselves knows that speaking to us about our future fills our hearts with faith and forms hope inside us. We believe what He has promised us is true, and so we step out in hope, suffering any pain necessary while we continue on, while we wait, even while we are ridiculed by others. This is how it was for Abraham:

> Against all hope, Abraham in hope believed and so became the father of many nations, just as it had been said to him, 'So shall your offspring be.' Without weakening in his faith, he faced the fact that his body was as good as dead—since he was about a hundred years old—and that Sarah's womb was also dead. Yet he did not waver through unbelief regarding the promise of God, but was strengthened in his faith and gave glory to God, being fully persuaded that God had power to do what he had promised (Romans 4:18-21).

When God made his promise to Abraham, since

> there was no one greater for Him to swear by, He swore by Himself, saying, 'I will surely bless you and give you many descendants.' And so after waiting patiently, Abraham received what was promised (Hebrews 6:13-15).

When you know what God has called you to do, you have an internal, constant incentive that pulls you closer and closer to Jesus. You wake up early in the morning to spend time at the beginning of your day with Him. You follow Him closely into and throughout their day. You listen constantly for Him to speak to you, to direct you, knowing that every moment of every day matters and that you are preparing for something—something wonderful. You "arm yourself" to suffer (see 1 Peter 4:1), just as Jesus did in order to continue on to your goal. You cry out to God to learn to live in the power of the Holy Spirit, knowing that your own capacity won't be enough for this God-sized, God-designed task before you.

Knowing your purpose fills your life with purpose. Every breath. Every word you read. Every obstacle you face. Every person you meet. Everything becomes "on purpose." Vision is a gift of God that helps you and requires you to walk closely with God, resulting in His life filling your own.

2. You grow in your ability and necessity to hear and obey God's voice.

Habakkuk 2:1-3 says,

> "I will stand at my watch and station myself on the ramparts; I will look to see what he will say to me, and what answer I am to give to this complaint. Then the Lord replied: 'Write down the revelation and make it plain on tablets so that a herald may run with it. For the revelation awaits an appointed time; it speaks of the end and will not prove false. Though it linger, wait for it; it will certainly come and will not delay.'"

You have to hear God tell you about our purpose and then, once you do, you need to hear Him tell you how to fulfill it. So you "station yourselves on the ramparts" and you "look to see what He will say to" you. Not only do you have to hear Him, but you have to learn to confirm what He has said. After all, you are banking your life on these words. Hearing God speak about your purpose isn't just a momentary thing. It requires waiting, shifting, following, and making decisions, and it requires a continued, constant hearing.

What God says about your purpose may require you to change majors in college, change jobs, to marry (or not marry) someone. Your quest to fulfill your purpose will take up the years of your life. You need to clearly and constantly hear Him and know that you know you are hearing Him. As a result, finding and fulfilling your purpose becomes an academy for learning to hear God's voice and obey it.

3. You will live in moment-to-moment intimacy in a deeper way.

Along with Abraham and Sarah, Moses is another great study of what happens for people called by God to a big purpose. In both stories, the individuals have to wrestle with God, to ask Him questions about what He has promised, and to even share their doubts and fears along the way. In Exodus 34:12-16, we get a glimpse of what this process was like for Moses:

> "Moses said to the Lord, 'You have been telling me, 'Lead these people,' but you have not let me know whom you will send with me. You have said, 'I know you by name and you have found favor with me.' If you are pleased with me, teach me your ways so I may know you and continue to find favor with you. Remember that this nation is your people.'
>
> The Lord replied, 'My Presence will go with you, and I will give you rest.'
>
> Then Moses said to him, 'If your Presence does not go with us, do not send us up from here. How will anyone know that you are pleased with me and with your people unless you go with us? What else will distinguish me and your people from all the other people on the face of the earth?'"

Moses, facing the challenging next steps in God's purpose

for His life, turned to God to ask for the help he needed in order to do what he has to do. In response to Moses' request for help, God told him that His presence will accompany Moses, that He Himself would be with Moses as he went. Moses quickly jumped at the offer, saying that if God didn't send His presence with him, he didn't want to go.

God's purpose for your life is a God-sized task that requires God's presence with you if you're to have any chance of success. Obedience is easiest in the presence of God. When you know in your heart that He is next to you, it's easy to obey and hard to disobey. However, facing the challenges that come with God leading you into His purposes for your life requires you to grow deeper and deeper in your commitment to seek His Presence in your life and to stay close to Him throughout your days.

4. You live by faith, even in the face of suffering.

Training for any great task requires rigor. In the movie, *Rocky*, the Italian heavyweight contender and underdog is continually pushed by his trainer, Mickey, to chase chickens to increase his agility, to do exercises to get him in shape, and to spar with other fighters to ready himself to face the champion. Mickey tells Rocky at one point that, "For a 45-minute fight, you gotta train hard for 45,000 minutes. 45,000! That's ten weeks, that's ten hours a day, ya listenin'? And you ain't even trained one!"[8] Training occurs when we endure difficult things—things that even require pain—as part of our preparation for doing whatever it will take to fulfill our calling or purpose.

Jesus calls you to be His disciples and within the word "disciple" you find a clue as to what it will take. The word "disciple" is tied to the word "discipline," and to be "discipled" or "disciplined" is really to be trained. God directs you to a life lived in the power of the Holy Spirit, devoted to hearing and obeying His voice. You are required to stay close to Him moment to moment regardless of the cost, the discomfort, the circumstances, or outer appearance. He deepens your faith, strengthens your hope, and leads you more and more deeply into living in His love.

As you grow, you will face more challenges and deeper

suffering but by staying close to Him, you won't even notice much of it. Jesus promises that following Him will be a tough road:

> "Then you will be handed over to be persecuted and put to death, and you will be hated by all nations because of me. At that time many will turn away from the faith and will betray and hate each other, and many false prophets will appear and deceive many people. Because of the increase of wickedness, the love of most will grow cold, but the one who stands firm to the end will be saved" (Matthew 24:9-12).

There at the end, is the payoff, the essential key: "But the one who stands firm to the end will be saved." Learning to live by faith through pain while you pursue your purpose develops in you a capacity to stand firm even to the end.

5. You live in His power as you pursue your purpose.

It's a common human tendency to avoid risk. We do this by staying within our own capabilities in situations that we can control. If there's a chance of failure or loss in any endeavor, many people won't try it. But the result of this is the tendency to live small lives.

When God speaks to you about your purpose, He speaks out of who He is, out of the mystery and majesty of His eternal counsel and purposes and in view of who He made you to be. Most often, He speaks about things that require a maturing faith in order to step into obedience and to do His will.

1. He told Noah to build a boat when it had never rained (see Genesis 6:13-18).

2. Abraham received one seemingly crazy direction after another.

3. Moses, a fugitive who was running from the law and who had moved from Pharaoh's palace to the fields where he cared for his father-in-law's livestock, was told to go and confront the most powerful ruler in the world (see Exodus 3-4).

4. A young shepherd boy named David was told by a visiting stranger that he would be king one day (1 Samuel 16:1-13).

5. A disoriented remnant of disciples were told they would do greater miracles than the Son of God once they received the Holy Spirit (see John 14:12).

When Jesus calls us, without exception He promises and provides power: "When Jesus had called the Twelve together, he gave them power and authority to drive out all demons and to cure diseases" (Luke 9:1) and again in Acts 1:8, "But you will receive power when the Holy Spirit comes on you; and you will be my witnesses in Jerusalem, and in all Judea and Samaria, and to the ends of the earth."

More specifically, the Father, Jesus, and the Holy Spirit work together to supply you with everything you need to step into God's purposes for your life. Peter, who himself experienced both the call of God and then His power to accompany it, wrote in 2 Peter 1:3, "His divine power has given us everything we need for a godly life through our knowledge of him who called us by his own glory and goodness."

Many people talk of wanting to see God's power while they cling to the "safety" and "assurance" of making their choices to do things within their own control and vision. But there's no need for God's power there. It's when you set out into the deep, challenging, faith-requiring steps toward the God-sized vision that He calls you to that you need Him. When you join Him in His purposes, you're given a front row seat to see Him demonstrate His power to accomplish what He has asked you to do for His glory.

God's purpose for your life is really important and likely much bigger than you can imagine. As you pursue a purpose journey with Him, your greatest reward will be getting to be with your Father who knit you together and laid out these purposes with the foundation of the Earth. Finding and fulfilling His purpose for your life will fill you with joy, peace, and the assurance that you have given yourself in the best possible way for the most critical thing you could possibly do. It won't be without difficulty, and there will be confusing moments. Purpose is what makes enduring them possible. Press in to Him and onward into the journey. It will be worth it.

CHAPTER 19

HOW TO FIND AND FULFILL GOD'S PURPOSE FOR YOUR LIFE?

So, you are made for one specific thing in the whole world. Only you can fulfill His purpose for you, and only God knows what it is. How will you go about finding and then fulfilling this one purpose He has given you? It can seem daunting and overwhelming. It can be the exact and only thing that consumes your heart. It can also be both of those things at once. Remember that God isn't trying to trick you, and He doesn't play games with your heart. He wants you to be living out your purpose more than you do. He's eager to launch into this journey with you, and He will give you everything you need in order to accomplish it. You'll find and fulfill God's purpose for your life in steps of hearing and acting in obedience. Before anything, you were made for a relationship with Him. As you draw closer to Him, He'll speak to you. He'll give you big vision that can be fulfilled through small steps of obedience. Respond to both. The following eight steps are helpful tools for finding and fulfilling God's purpose for your life.

1. Believe that God is good and means good for you every day of your life.

The truth is that knowing God, living in an intimate friendship with Him, and being in His presence would be more than enough for you to lead and enjoy an amazing life. Yet your faith levels aren't strong enough to allow you to get in on these things. You have to grow in faith to do so. God invites you to embark on a journey to discover and fulfill His purposes for your life as a place where you're forced to learn who He is and His ways, and to deepen your trust in Him with each step.

Every day requires you to hear Him, to respond to His call and trust Him. One thing that can help you thrive on this journey is to begin with a bold confidence that the God who calls you or sends you is a good God who intends to demonstrate His love for you and deepen your trust in Him each step of the way. You'll face challenging times that will put this trust to the test again and again. If you remember His goodness and that He loves you, you have a better chance of not turning back.

2. Take up your cross, deny yourself, and follow Him. Pay attention to the name of this forgotten piece.

It's not "Finding and Fulfilling Your Purpose for your Life." It's "Finding and Fulfilling His Purpose for Your Life." If you want to get a hold of His purpose, you can't bring your ways with you. Taking up your cross, denying yourself, and following Him is the only way to be free from your own thoughts and hear His voice tell you His big vision. It's the only way to have access to the faith it will require to stand in the midst of a world chasing the fleeting high of self-satisfaction, deny what is sensical and reasonable to you, and move when He says to move.

You can't take hold of your purpose without surrendering to Jesus. You can't get there without the resurrection power that comes when your old, dead heart is made alive in Him. And though this is the counter-intuitive part, this is actually the secret key. There's no way to find His purpose (which leads to a great, powerful, intentional, romantic, abundant experience with Him) until you surrender anything you've built on your own.

Purpose is a critical reason you surrender it all to Him in the first place: to know with complete confidence what you were made for and to be entirely free to do whatever it will take to get there and experience it all. At the cross is resurrection power, His Holy Spirit everywhere, on the move. It's where you'll find everything you need to live freely in your powerful, purposeful life, with the driving force of faith pushing you onward toward His purpose.

3. Ask Him. Seek Him. Listen to Him.

The secret to finding your purpose in life is to ask God. This requires you to hear His voice and to obey what He says. One of the benefits of this pathway to your purpose is that it forces you to learn to hear Him and to grow stronger and stronger in learning to respond to what He says. Jesus teaches you how to approach God for the things you want and need from Him. He tells you to ask, to seek, and to knock, knowing that as a good Father, God will listen and answer you:

> "Ask and it will be given to you; seek and you will find; knock and the door will be opened to you. For everyone who asks receives; the one who seeks finds; and to the one who knocks, the door will be opened. Which of you, if your son asks for bread, will give him a stone? Or if he asks for a fish, will give him a snake? If you, then, though you are evil, know how to give good gifts to your children, how much more will your Father in heaven give good gifts to those who ask him!" (Matthew 7:7-11).

Ask, seek, knock, and be ready because He will respond.

4. Pay attention and follow up on every clue.

In the early stages of seeking God for your purpose, purchase a journal or notebook specifically for recording clues that you uncover each day, and write them down. When you see a movie that has a character doing something or working in a job that thrills your heart, write it down. This could be a clue about what God has created you to do.

Constantly ask people to talk about their dreams or their work—what God has called them to do. Listen for things they say that cause your heart to burn within you. Write those things down as well. Sort through what you enjoy and what you don't enjoy. Do you enjoy reading? Writing? Math? Science? Write it down. Do you enjoy working with a lot of people all day? Do you enjoy working alone? As you talk through these things with others or even contemplate them on your own, write down every clue you come to.

5. Adjust your course according to even the smallest clue.

Regardless of who you are or how old you are, this is a perfect example of how important it is to have a coach. Turn to the person God has given you as a coach or mentor and ask them what they see in you. Write these things down and also show your coach all the clues you've written down. Then, together try to identify patterns. Pray and ask God to help you identify opportunities based on the patterns you see emerging.

If you see, hear, or sense that you're made to care for people, volunteer with various nonprofit organizations or ministries; see which activities fill your heart with joy and which do not. If you're a student and you love math, take a minute to talk to your favorite math teacher. Ask them what kind of jobs are available for people who are good at math. Spend time with a doctor or nurse and get a sense of whether you're made for helping people in the medical field. Spend time with a lawyer to see if your way of helping people might be in their line of work.

As you go, listen. The Holy Spirit will actually show you when you're "getting warmer" or "getting colder." Write down each clue (your experience, the parts that stood out, the parts that bored you, etc.) and continually discuss what you're hearing with your coach and your team or small group. God will speak through the people around you, and as He speaks even a little bit, take the next step toward what He says. Be ready for surprises, and be ready for action.

6. Remember that your purpose isn't a job but a calling.

While the pathway to purpose requires you to turn over every rock and search high and low, including thinking through academic strengths and occupational fit, it's important to remember that your calling is bigger than a job. Your calling will be lived out through all your life, including your job, but not limited to it. There can be real strength when what you do for a living at least fits in with your calling, but be prepared for God's creativity here. Many people's purposes are more of a dynamic or value that can be expressed in almost any area of their lives.

Your purpose might be to "extract the precious from the worthless," and you might continually see value in people and situations where others don't, so God uses you to grab hold of what appears worthless in a person or a moment and encourages the beauty He reveals in them. Your purpose might be to "bring order out of chaos," so your life may continually be about administrating situations where you start with a great deal of disorder, or mentoring people who are scattered in many ways, but, little by little, you help make things better.

You might be called to develop young people or to help people grow into their God-given purpose or calling. You might be called to serve a specific people group like children in foster care or those who are fatherless. None of these things are encompassed by one occupation. Actually, these things can be accomplished in any vocation where there are people. Be open. Be attentive. Don't limit what He might say to you. Be ready to be wowed by what God made you for, and be ready to follow Him with your whole heart into fulfilling it.

7. Don't turn back when the seas get choppy.

Expect to encounter His power to help you. In the beginning, these steps into what you're sensing from the Lord will be pretty low risk and low cost. With each morsel of clarity, you'll be forced to commit a bit more to step into what He's saying. Along the way, even as you get clearer and clearer, you'll face obstacles, challenges, and difficulties. At times, these circumstances might be God's way of telling you that you've taken a wrong turn. Yet be careful here. Many times, the difficult road can be an indicator that you're actually on the right path and that God is working your faith muscles to learn how to lean on Him and see His power help you overcome what you face.

Like Abraham, your purpose isn't something you'll be able to do in your own strength. It's something that will require you to build a friendship with God that will cause you to depend on His power and strength. You'll need to hear Him. You'll need to know that *you know* that you've heard Him. You'll be forced to suffer or stand in the midst of adversity and to hold on to the hope of God's calling on your life. If you do, your life will change the course of history and leave a legacy of faith and obedience that will touch many other lives.

8. Watch how your calling or mission fits into Jesus's ongoing mission.

Jesus came to "seek and save the lost." He came to lay His life down as a sacrifice so that we could receive forgiveness for our sins, and redemption, being restored to a relationship with the Father. After dying and being resurrected, Jesus ascended into heaven where He sits at the right hand of the Father and where He's waiting for all things in heaven and on earth to be placed under His feet, under His Kingdom rule. At that point, He will turn and hand everything to the Father.

This mission of Jesus' is ongoing. Whatever you're called to do with your life plays a part in His mission. There's no question that your calling is a part of His call to reach people with the gospel (the good news of His love and pursuit of them). Just as you have been, there are many others out there who sense something in their hearts drawing them to God.

In your calling, He'll bring people (customers, coworkers, friends) close to you whom you can love. He will speak words into your heart that will draw them home. God will give you influence that will allow you to do what He says in your workplace, family, relationships, or community, allowing His Kingdom rule to be expressed in these spaces. As this happens, you take part in everything being placed under His feet. Your calling fits within His calling and weaves your life into His eternal purposes.

This **forgotten piece** is exciting and a necessary part of your life. You'll need to know what you were made for in order to live a life of faith. You'll want to know your purpose in order to grow, help others, and satiate the desires of your heart. Finding and fulfilling His purpose for your life is a lifelong pursuit. He doesn't waste days or words. It will be an exciting journey, and you'll do great things with His help and leading. Remember, you were made first for Him—to be with Him, know Him, and be known by Him. Stay close to your Father. Listen to every word He says. Look for Him in every part of your day. Choose Him even if it's difficult or doesn't make sense to you. As you do these things, you'll uncover His purpose for your life.

CHAPTER 20

FINDING AND FULFILLING GOD'S PURPOSE FOR YOUR LIFE: A SUMMARY

It is God's nature to give purpose. He doesn't waste anything—words, moments, or a single thing from your life. You're alive and given each day because He has purposed you for something specific that only you can do.

This **forgotten piece** is most likely part of the reason you turned to God in the first place. This idea that you were made to do something, to give your heart and life for something, to participate in meaningful and helpful change for the world, is the reason to get out of bed in the morning.

Your purpose won't come in a one-hour prayer session. Your purpose will be revealed and lived out through every moment of every day with Him. The more you uncover your purpose, the more you'll need to be close to Him. The closer you are to Him, the more you'll learn about your purpose. So the purpose journey goes.

Throughout this section, we looked at Abraham's life, the father of our faith and the follower of His promises. We shared our own stories and laid out the reasons why and the ways you can find and fulfill God's purpose for your life. Why learn to find and fulfill God's purpose for your life?

1. Your life is filled with vision.
2. You grow in your ability and necessity to hear and obey God's voice.
3. You live in moment-to-moment intimacy in a deeper way.
4. You live by faith, even in the face of suffering.
5. You live in His power as you pursue His purpose.

How do you find and fulfill God's purpose for your life?

1. Believe that God is good and means good for you every day of your life.
2. Take up your cross, deny yourself, and follow Him.
3. Ask Him. Seek Him. Listen to Him.
4. Pay attention and follow up on every clue.
5. Adjust your course according to even the smallest clue.
6. Remember that your purpose isn't a job but a calling.
7. Don't turn back when the seas get choppy.
8. Watch how your calling or mission fits into Jesus' ongoing mission.

You were made on purpose for a purpose that was laid out by a God who created you, the universe, and everything else. You were not skipped over, given a lesser part, or missed. You were purposed, and God cares a great deal about sharing every intimate detail of it with you. Believe you were given a purpose. Obey Him when you hear Him speak. This vision He will give you will take you on an amazing journey. You will get to see things, say things, and do things that you can't yet imagine, and He'll use you to participate in the redemption of broken, painful places in spaces in people's hearts and around the world. Don't wait to get in on it.

LIVING LIFE IN THE POWER OF THE HOLY SPIRIT

"But you will receive power when the Holy Spirit has come upon you; and you shall be My witnesses both in Jerusalem, and in all Judea and Samaria, and even to the remotest part of the earth" (Acts 1:8).

CHAPTER 21

PETER: FROM THE REED TO THE ROCK

Every superhero's story includes the moment when they go from being an everyday, ordinary person to someone who receives extraordinary, supernatural power. Before that transformation, these characters struggled to handle their own problems and lives. And then a bite from a radioactive spider or exposure to a supernatural element launches them from a life of weakness to a life with enough power to help the entire world.

In the "origin stories" we read of regular people in the Bible, we see how they are powerfully altered by meeting God and learning to walk with Him. We saw this in Samuel, in John, and in Abraham. Without Him, they were in big trouble. With Him, they did great things.

Still the crescendo of the story laid out in the Bible comes when Jesus demonstrates miraculous, seemingly impossible power, because He's filled with and led by the Holy Spirit. He promises the gift of the same Holy Spirit to us. Not only are followers of Jesus invited into a relationship with Him, and through Him with the Father, but He promises that the third person of the Trinity, the Holy Spirit, will baptize or fill them and then lead them into lives that will "turn the world upside down."

The Apostle Peter, one of Jesus' earliest and closest disciples, was first a reed and then a rock. In fact, when Peter first met Jesus, his name wasn't Peter but Simon. The name "Simon" in Hebrew means "a reed," a plant that sways back and forth in the wind. From outward appearance, Simon Peter was a strong, gregarious fisherman. In fact, it was Simon's brother and partner in the fishing business, Andrew, who introduced him to Jesus.

While Simon was a husband, a strong outdoorsman, and businessman who made his living through physical labor, we see in the gospels that even strong people can waver back and forth when it comes to making important choices. Simon Peter's intense personality, rapid reactions, and slowly-developing faith made him quick to act without deeper wisdom and, as a result, quick to make mistakes.

Even after Simon had already met Him, Jesus needed to do a miracle of catching an amazing amount of fish to help this fisherman see that He is the Son of God, the Messiah. Prior to the big catch, Simon nonchalantly addressed Jesus as "teacher" while sarcastically explaining to Jesus that there was no reason to cast their nets again. Afterwards when they had an abundant catch, Simon cried out for Jesus, whom he then addressed as "Lord," to get away from him because he was unclean. Within a few minutes, Simon left behind the boats to follow the Jesus he had just doubted.

Many are familiar with the story of Jesus calling Simon Peter to get up out of the boat in which he was traveling and come to Him by walking on the water (see Matthew 14:22-33). Simon responded with inspirational faith, actually walking on water until his faith began to waver, and he began to sink. Within just a few moments, Simon went from launching himself into a miracle to losing his confidence, needing to be rescued.

The stories continue throughout the gospel accounts, including one jaw-dropping instance in Matthew 16. Jesus asked His disciples who they think He is, to which Simon Peter answered so well that Jesus said,

"Blessed are you, Simon son of Jonah, for this

was not revealed to you by flesh and blood, but by my Father in heaven. And I tell you that you are Peter, and on this rock I will build my church, and the gates of Hades will not overcome it. I will give you the keys of the kingdom of heaven; whatever you bind on earth will be bound in heaven, and whatever you loose on earth will be loosed in heaven" (Matthew 16:17-19).

It's here that Jesus prophetically looked into Peter's eyes and heart and changed his name: No longer would he be a weak, wishy-washy reed, being pushed around and flipped by circumstance and internal pressures. His name would be Peter, meaning "a rock." Where he was once flimsy, he would now be solid.

And yet just a few lines down the page, Peter already flip-flopped to the point that Jesus was forced to issue one of His strongest recorded rebukes: "Jesus turned and said to Peter, 'Get behind me, Satan! You are a stumbling block to me; you do not have in mind the concerns of God, but merely human concerns'" (Matthew 16:23).

At one of the most important points in history, Peter, one of Jesus's three closest disciples due to his emerging "rock-like" characteristics, lost faith in a very public manner, denying Jesus three times just a few hours after telling his Master that he was willing to lay down his life for Him.

Yet, thank God, this wasn't the end of the story. Even though Jesus publicly changed his name, Simon, the reed, wasn't able to change himself from being a weak and inconsistent follower of the Savior that he so passionately loved. Even after three years of having one of the closest seats to Jesus' life, His miracles, His words. Even after a litany of rebukes, of corrections, and of Jesus working on Peter's character, he remained a reed in his actions, unable to live in the firmness and strength to which Jesus was so clearly calling Him.

And then, just when you think Peter's story would end in sadness and defeat, one of the world's most important miracles happened. Days after Jesus' crucifixion and resurrection, He came to reinstate Peter to apostleship. After that, He told all of the disciples to stay together and wait for Him to send His Helper. Then in the upper room of a house filled with Jesus' followers, the Holy Spirit arrived for them.

It was the coming of the Holy Spirit that changed Peter into a true rock while simultaneously establishing the Church Peter would help lead:

> When the day of Pentecost came, they were all together in one place. Suddenly a sound like the blowing of a violent wind came from heaven and filled the whole house where they were sitting. They saw what seemed to be tongues of fire that separated and came to rest on each of them. All of them were filled with the Holy Spirit and began to speak in other tongues as the Spirit enabled them (Acts 2:1-4).

As a large crowd gathered, including many of the same people who had previously witnessed Peter denying Jesus, and they needed someone to explain to them what that moment meant. Peter, then filled with the Holy Spirit, stood and preached one of the most important messages ever shared. The result was the beginning of a movement that has lasted for more than 2,000 years and which I trust you're part of today: "Those who accepted his message were baptized, and about three thousand were added to their number that day" (Acts 2:41).

Much of Peter's story centers on helping more and more people hear about Jesus, believe in Him, choose to follow Him, and then receive the gift of the Holy Spirit. For Peter, the Holy Spirit is the Difference-Maker, the Helper, the Comforter. The Holy Spirit is the One who enabled and em-powered him to hear God's voice more clearly and to obey it, to live in God's presence, and to overcome obstacles and adversity to carry out his God-given mission or purpose.

Peter learned the importance of the Holy Spirit while be-ing an eyewitness to the place the Holy Spirit had in Jesus' own ministry. Prior to doing any miracles, when Jesus was baptized in water by His cousin, John the Baptist, the Holy Spirit descended like a dove to baptize Him in the Spirit, too. Jesus was then led by the Spirit into the wilderness for an extended time of fasting and praying, "full of the Holy Spirit." Immediately after, He returned, entered a syn-agogue, and read Isaiah 61:1:

"The Spirit of the Sovereign Lord is on me, because the Lord has anointed me to proclaim
good news to the poor. He has sent me to bind
up the brokenhearted, to proclaim freedom for
the captives and release from darkness for the
prisoners" (also see Matthew 4:1-17).

In one of Jesus' final conversations with the disciples,
He shared with them the power and promise of the Holy
Spirit. He explained it would be better for them that He go
because He would then ask the Father to give them this
powerful gift (see John 16:7), and the Holy Spirit would
come into their hearts and lives. He would convict them
when they weren't responding to Jesus' voice, His ways,
His heart. He would remind them of what Jesus had already
said to them. He would lead them into the full depth of
God's purposes for their lives.

We are followers of Jesus to the extent that we are currently following Jesus. He invites us not just to accept Him
as a wise teacher or even as someone who cleans up our
mistakes from the past, but as the *Lord* and *King* of our
lives. The intimate, constantly interactive relationship we
see before the Fall in the Garden, where Adam and Eve
walked and talked with God each day, what we see in
Abraham learning to live with God across his journey, and
then in the life that Jesus lives in dependence on Father by
being filled with and yielding to the direction of the Holy
Spirit—that is what we are made to live as well. We can't
follow Jesus without receiving the Holy Spirit and learning
to live our lives according to His direction and in His power.

Today, the version of Christianity that includes singing
beautiful songs in comfortable auditoriums, listening to
good messages and reading nice verses in our Bibles is
losing the next generation because it's missing the power
of the Holy Spirit. Somehow, even the most lost and broken heart knows there must be something more. The original group of believers who received the power of the Holy
Spirit on the same day that Peter changed from a reed to
a rock was soon described as those "who have turned the
world upside down" (Acts 17:6).

In Acts 2 when the Holy Spirit came down on this original

group of Jesus' followers, the Church was formed. It was the indwelling presence of the Holy Spirit that transformed Peter and turned a seemingly random gathering of people into the *body of Christ*. Just as the Holy Spirit came into Jesus to fill, guide, and empower Him for life-changing ministry and miracles, the Holy Spirit comes into our lives today to fill, guide and empower us to love those God brings close to us.

As we recapture these pieces, as we receive this gift of the Holy Spirit and learn to walk in His power, we too will see a new generation come to believe and follow Jesus. We too will learn to live lives that turn the world upside down.

The Holy Spirit is called the Helper (see John 14:26). He's constantly on the move—working all things together for our good. We don't want to live our lives without the Helper; we can't live effective lives without Him. As we explore this last **forgotten piece** in the following chapters, there will be stories and more reasons why and ways to live in the power of the Holy Spirit. Know this as you begin: The Holy Spirit will lead you into a miraculous, God-defined life. He'll give you words, ideas, hope, and help, and He's the one who will accomplish God's will for you. The Holy Spirit makes every other **forgotten piece** possible, and this forgotten piece will change your life in absolutely amazing ways.

CHAPTER 22

A GLIMPSE AT LIVING OUR LIVES IN THE POWER OF THE HOLY SPIRIT

As a young youth pastor, I was blessed to be connected to two leaders who recognized God's calling on my life and continually invested in sending me to go and be with people who could help me grow. One summer, I was sent to intern with the youth ministry of a vibrant inner-city church in Pittsburgh, Pennsylvania. Close to the end of the internship and just at the end of a weekend conference, the youth pastor and evangelism pastor of the church grabbed me and led me up a staircase into a small classroom to meet a mother and her 16-year-old daughter.

The daughter, who seemed very sad and a little angry,

sat at a desk as the four of us—the two pastors, the mom and myself—stood around her. The evangelism pastor said, "Let's pray." With an uncharacteristic boldness, I interrupted to ask, "Excuse me. Could you tell me what we are praying for?" The man gestured to the mother to explain. "My daughter doesn't want to listen to me. She isn't doing well, and I won't put up with it." I was new at knowing how to hear God speak to me but as the mother spoke, I heard Him clearly say, "The problem isn't just the daughter."

The men began to pray the kind of religious prayers that pastors sometimes pray when their hearts aren't connected to what they're praying for: "Lord, help this young girl listen to what her mom is saying to her..." The more they prayed, the more my heart began to feel something I had never felt before. I had only known Jesus and been filled with the Holy Spirit for a few years. I was very new at hearing God's voice. However, I could feel an intense sense of injustice rising up in me as we prayed. Something had to be done or said differently. There I was a young intern, surrounded by experienced men of God and a woman who was clearly my elder. As the tension increased, I wasn't sure what to do or what to say.

Finally, it was my turn to pray. I couldn't stop myself from interrupting the prayer and turning to the girl to say, "I feel like God wants to tell you that you're not a problem. You're a princess. It takes a special young woman to even walk into this room and to sit here as we pray for you. Many young people wouldn't be willing to suffer through this. Every young person struggles at times to relate to their parents. That doesn't make you a problem." I then prayed and the others began to pray differently, too. I had sensed something by the power of the Holy Spirit, acted on it, and I watched how the Holy Spirit changed everything.

As we said, "Amen," the girl launched herself out of the little desk and into my arms as she burst into tears. I hugged her for a moment, and then a miracle happened. She pushed me back and ran into her mom's arms as the two women fell to the floor, both crying. I could hear the mother saying, again and again, "I'm so sorry, baby. I am so sorry."

Tears flooded down my face, and I turned and walked out of the room, saying to the Lord, "Jesus, please let me be a part of doing that over and over again in my life."

CHAPTER 23

WHY LIVE IN THE POWER OF THE HOLY SPIRIT?

The Holy Spirit was so important that Jesus told the disciples they couldn't do anything, not to even try to do anything, until the Spirit came. He made them wait for the Spirit before they could go out to live their lives of faith. It's a critical discipline for you, too, to follow the leading of the Holy Spirit into your life. The Holy Spirit changes everything. He provides intel and a constant connection to the voice of God. He'll give you creative ideas that you would never have otherwise. He'll help you help others in ways that last. Living your life in the power of the Holy Spirit means you won't live your life in your own power or in the power of the world. You'll have constant access to God's power and God's ways. Living your life in the power of the Holy Spirit frees you from your best efforts and launches you into a life you were made for. The following are seven reasons why.

1. You were made for life in the Spirit.

There's a long list of things that we believe we need in

order to be happy: *If I can just meet the person I will fall in love with, and who will fall in love with me. If I can just graduate from school and get a great job. If I just make a lot of money. If I can be famous and known.* Even deeper than those things are the **forgotten pieces** set out in this book: Hearing His voice. Living in His presence. Knowing His calling for our lives and then stepping into it.

While several of these things are keys to knowing and being close to the God who created you, they all set up the final of the **forgotten pieces**. You were created by God, who is spirit, to live a life full of and led by the Holy Spirit. While you can't get to life in the Holy Spirit without hearing and obeying His voice, His voice is a spiritual voice calling you to a Spirit-led life. Living in moment-to-moment intimacy with God is a key to living life in the Holy Spirit. However, if you were to practice His presence with all diligence but come up short of encountering the power of the Holy Spirit in your daily life, you would fall short of what you were created for.

You were created by the Powerful One, Elohim, the Creator of all things, whose Holy Spirit hovered over the depths and formed everything that exists. You were called to be a disciple of Jesus, who demonstrated what life in the Holy Spirit can be, performing one jaw-dropping, game-changing miracle after another. You were made to be among those who would continue a movement that exploded into existence in the book of Acts. Everyday men and women, fishermen, merchants, brothers, mothers, and daughters were filled with the Holy Spirit and in short order turned the world upside down. You were made to live the same way, and you won't be satisfied with anything less.

2. You get what Jesus promised you.

Jesus spoke to His disciples about the promise of the Holy Spirit (Beginning in John 14 and ending in John 16). He laid out a list of ways we would benefit from the Holy Spirit coming into our lives:

- **A shepherd within us.** "But the Advocate, the Holy Spirit, whom the Father will send in my name, will teach you all things and will remind you of everything I have said to you" (John 14:26). Jesus promised that the Holy Spirit will teach you everything you need to know and remind you of all that Jesus has said. He'll continually shepherd you, guiding you through every challenge of your life.

- **He shows us Jesus.** "When the Advocate comes, whom I will send to you from the Father—the Spirit of truth who goes out from the Father—he will testify about me" (John 15:26). It's difficult to imagine a greater promise than having the Holy Spirit, one person of the Trinity, living within you and telling you about Jesus, inviting you closer to Him every moment of your life. The Holy Spirit continually leads you closer to Jesus, who continually leads you closer to the Father.

- **He shows us what is not Jesus**. "When he comes, he will prove the world to be in the wrong about sin and righteousness and judgment" (John 16:8). When Jesus died in your place on the Cross, He destroyed condemnation and your sentence to severe punishment for your mistakes and shortcomings. His death satisfied the death sentence your sins require. There's therefore no condemnation, but in its place you find the very useful tool of conviction. The Holy Spirit, Jesus promises, convicts your heart and conscience of an actions that are outside of God's will.

As you head into your daily life, get tired or tempted, begin to disconnect from Jesus, and choose lesser things, the Holy Spirit sets off an internal alarm, warning you that you're getting further away from Jesus and need to turn around. At the same time, only the Holy Spirit can and will convince other people where they're making decisions that lead them far from God and will bring devastating consequences. Your job isn't to set others right, keep track of their errors, or scream at them about their mistakes. You're to love and serve people, and it's the Holy Spirit who will accomplish justice, set everything right, and make everyone clean.

- **An embedded guidance system.** "But when he, the Spirit of truth, comes, he will guide you into all the truth. He will not speak on his own; he will speak only what he hears, and he will tell you what is yet to come. He will glorify me because it is from me that he will receive what he will make known to you. All that belongs to the Father is mine. That is why I said the Spirit will receive from me what he will make known to you" (John 16:13-15). The Holy Spirit will provide you with a supernatural guidance system, search engine, and supercomputer all in one. Embedded in your heart and mind to give you insight, the Holy Spirit gives guidance and power as you live your life and love others.

  The prophet Isaiah foretold this gift in Isaiah 30: 20-21 when he wrote, "Although the Lord gives you the bread of adversity and the water of affliction, your teachers will be hidden no more; with your own eyes you will see them. Whether you turn to the right or to the left, your ears will hear a voice behind you, saying, 'This is the way; walk in it.'" Jesus actually told the disciples that having the gift of the Holy Spirit within them would be even more helpful than having Jesus Himself there in the flesh. No longer would they be separated from God's wisdom, power and guidance. Never again would they, or now you, be helpless or lost. Even when you walk through difficulties and suffering, you'll still hear His voice and direction.

- **The power to accomplish your mission:** "Do not leave Jerusalem, but wait for the gift my Father promised, which you have heard me speak about. For John baptized with water, but in a few days you will be baptized with the Holy Spirit" (Acts 1:4-5). "But you will receive power when the Holy Spirit comes on you, and you will be my witnesses in Jerusalem, and in all Judea and Samaria, and to the ends of the earth" (Acts 1:8). You're not to get started until you receive this life-changing gift.

It's the Holy Spirit who provides you with the power to follow Jesus into reaching hurting people and drawing them to believe in Jesus. It's the Holy Spirit who empowers you to know Jesus and follow Him, becoming so dependent on Him that our own actions and lives captivate people as we interact with them. It's the Holy Spirit who performs miraculous acts, healing, helping, and revealing that He's the answer to their struggles and pain. It's the Holy Spirit who will guide your words to reach people's hearts, unlocking them to believe and choose to trust Jesus and follow Him. Without the Holy Spirit, you can do nothing. With Him, the same effective ministry you see in Jesus's life in the Gospels begins to flow through your life, both individually and alongside other believers that Jesus weaves you together with.

3. You get continuous access to the One who is greater than anything in the world.

There's nothing you'll ever encounter that can rival or come close to the power of the Holy Spirit. The same Spirit that raised Christ from the dead is now alive in us (see Romans 8:11). Knowing this, you build an altar with your life, story after story of faith-filled acts that change your life and the lives of others. Life in the power of the Holy Spirit is a worshipful life, a life free from the brokenness of the world, a life that's effective and impactful, that satisfies every empty, dry, forgotten place in your heart. You need only ask, and He is yours.

4. You become like Jesus.

There's a strange sounding word, *sanctification*, that's used across Church history that has little draw today. However, this word captures one of the most powerful and important aspects of what the gift of the Holy Spirit does in you: It is where the Holy Spirit leads you in each moment of your life deeper and deeper into a life of faith and communion with Jesus, recreating Jesus's personality, character, love, and life in our own. Sanctification literally means to set something apart for God's special use and purpose.

Yet you experience it in your life as the Holy Spirit's miraculous power identifies behaviors, thoughts, and desires that remain from before you knew Jesus. He then convicts you of these things and actually works into your heart the desire and capability to change. You aren't capable or called to change yourself. It's the Holy Spirit who leads you to be more and more led by Him, making you like Him—holy.

5. You receive comfort from God, the only comfort that satisfies your heart.

So much of what hurts you in life is where your heart is incomplete and unsatisfied, leaving you wide open to temptation to run after things that are not good for you. This dissatisfaction or the hunger and thirst within you is actually a spiritual symptom of the truth that you are made to live closer to God. The gift of the Holy Spirit is like a FedEx delivery driver who takes all of the love, peace, sweetness and affection that God created for you to receive from Him and brings it down into your life. As you learn to come close to the Holy Spirit, to relate to Him more and more intimately, and yield to His leading, you receive His comfort in ways that deeply satisfy and satiate your heart. It is in this way that you experience real peace— peace that surpasses understanding— with such depth that you know how loved you are, and that bubbles up into joy.

6. You gain access to the fruit and gifts of the Holy Spirit.

In the book of Galatians, in chapter 5, verses 22-23, Paul wrote a list of fruit or gifts of the Holy Spirit: "But the fruit of the Spirit is love, joy, peace, patience, kindness, goodness, faithfulness, gentleness and self-control." It's easy to read through this list and underestimate what each word offers. Our English definitions leave the impression that they're all very nice but not very exciting. However, if you dig deeper, this list is filled with revolutionary, life-changing power.

- Love—Love isn't just drawing red hearts next to someone's name and saying we will be best friends forever. It's more than a generic, utopian desire for treating every person with respect or even romance. The specific word for love is the Greek word "agape," and it is unlike any other love. It's a love that doesn't need to be loved back, that doesn't seek its own. It's love straight from God's heart that fills your life to the extent that you go out giving it without needing someone to do the same in return. It allows you to love the unlovely, to forgive, to be slapped across the face and rejected and to keep on loving. It's the love that Jesus Himself lived out in loving us while we were His enemies. It's a love that can reach into another person's brokenness and participate in God's rescue of their heart and life.

- Joy—The Greek word for joy is pretty close to the word "grace." It's defined as an awareness of God's grace and favor. It's actually to rejoice because of grace. It's joy that comes out of an awareness that Jesus is with you, loves you, and is extending His favor into each moment of your life.

- Peace—This isn't just peace that means tranquility or a cessation of violence. In Hebrew, this word is, "shalom," and it's speaks to more to the concept of wholeness. Shalom is a fullness of life, provision, love, justice, and everything a person or community could need.

- Patience—This is a quality of God. It's divinely-regulated patience which involves waiting sufficient time before expressing anger and avoiding the premature use of force to resolve things that rises out of improper anger. Patience is suffering well, not needing to resolve something that causes tension in order to give room for a person or situation to grow.

- Kindness—This is a big one. The Greek word "Xrestotes" means useable, what is truly needed, kindness that's actionable. It's useful kindness that meets real needs in God's timing and His way. Rather than "being nice," it's a Spirit-empowered goodness that produces effective help and isn't marred by human harshness.

- Goodness—The word "good" or "like God" describes what originates from God and is empowered by Him in a person's life through faith. The more you yield your life to the leadership of the Holy Spirit, the more your heart and life fill with His life and His power, or in other words, His goodness.

- Faith—As mentioned earlier, faith can be defined as hearing God's words spoken to your heart and trusting them to the point of responding with action. Faith is conversation with God that results in relationship and obedience. A life of faith is very much a gateway into life in the power of the Holy Spirit.

- Gentleness—Gentleness means gentle strength, power with reserve, meekness or strength under God's direction. Gentleness begins with the Holy Spirit's inspiration and finishes by His direction and empowerment. It's divinely-balanced virtue and can only operate through faith.

- Self-control—Self-control doesn't mean you're in control of yourself, but rather that you are effective at allowing yourself to be yielded to the Spirit's control. This can only be accomplished by the power of the Lord. This is why it's a fruit of the Holy Spirit.

7. You are healed and filled, and then, you overflow.

The Holy Spirit does constant, good, and effective work. Each of these reasons you need to learn to live your life in the power of the Holy Spirit only begin to detail the intimate care and freedom you will receive when the Spirit is at work in you. The feeling of being constantly let down by your life isn't wrong. You were not made to compromise yourself and settle for a broken heart and half-fulfilled dreams. No, the Lord is completely good, and even when there are difficult and painful moments where the Spirit is working out your sin to replace it with fruit, He means complete good for you. You'll be healed of every sin when you're filled with the Spirit. He simply won't leave any spot of darkness in your heart; the Spirit will relentlessly set you free until you're filled in every way with light.

As He does this work in you, He will overfill you, and you'll have something to give others to bring them into this life, too. The Spirit will fill you as He heals you. He will use you (even while you're still a work in progress) to change the lives of others. And you won't have to worry about having enough; the Spirit has plenty for every heart that yearns to leave sin and hurt behind for the miraculous, merciful, and complete work of God.

The Holy Spirit is the accomplisher of God's will in the world. Anything you set out to do in faith will require the power of the Holy Spirit. He isn't an optional add-on or a smaller character within the Trinity. The Holy Spirit is God's Spirit given to you so that it's possible for you to hear His voice and obey, live intimately connected to God, embrace a life of faith even when there's suffering, and find and fulfill your purpose. The Holy Spirit is the same spirit that raised Christ from the dead, and He's at work in you (see Romans 6:10-11).

CHAPTER 24

HOW DO YOU LIVE IN THE POWER OF THE HOLY SPIRIT?

The Holy Spirit doesn't work according to what you find reasonable or sensible. The Holy Spirit isn't limited by you, even though He does live and work within you. The Holy Spirit is God's Spirit forever moving towards accomplishing God's will. Learning to live in His power and ways will take some time, because it will be counterintuitive to what is natural to you. He will help you (He is after all, called the Helper), and you'll grow. Learning to live your life in the power of the Holy Spirit is an exciting and essential learning process that will impact every single part of your life. This chapter focuses on six ways to learn how.

1. Take up your cross, deny yourself, and follow Him.

Again, you learn this from your how-to guide. Jesus isn't

an example for your life; Jesus is *the* example for your life. Jesus waited until the time that God appointed for Him to go into ministry, and before He went, He was baptized first in water and then in the Holy Spirit. He lived in constant dependence upon the Father and the power of the Holy Spirit. It's much simpler than we make it out to be. Jesus is our example, and He tells you what's required: take up your cross, deny yourself, and follow Him.

He's your example that you follow. And here's a secret: It requires the work of the Holy Spirit for you to recognize that your own life and your own ways won't work. The Holy Spirit is necessary for you to even want His ways. In fact, the Holy Spirit is necessary for anything in your life to bear fruit.

To the extent that you experience the cross, and to the extent that you yourself are broken at the cross, is the extent to which you will experience the power of Pentecost—the power of resurrection. Though it will feel counterintuitive, it is both what you want and what you desperately need.

2. Be water baptized.

Jesus was filled with the Holy Spirit right after being baptized in water. There's a reason for this. When you are water baptized, you lay down your old life—the life lived apart and independent from God, the way the world lives. When Adam and Eve pulled away from God to follow the enemy's voice, mankind, and creation with them, fell into lives disconnected from God, dead to His voice, dead to His life, and dead to His will. While you weren't made to live this way and it brings immediate death with it, God has given humans the freedom to choose it. It's horrible. It's a rejection of God, His goodness, and His place in your lives and, as a result, a rejection of the forgiveness Jesus has purchased for you with His death on the cross.

Baptism in water is your decision, made for all the natural and spiritual world to see, declaring that you are laying down your whole life, burying it under the waters of baptism so that you can be raised with Jesus again, born into a new life with Him— the way God intended you to live. Paul details the power of being baptized in water in Romans 6:3-4:

> "Or don't you know that all of us who were baptized into Christ Jesus were baptized into

his death? We were therefore buried with him through baptism into death so that, just as Christ was raised from the dead through the glory of the Father, we too may live a new life."

Paul goes on to say that by dying "with Christ" we now "live with Him." The death and disconnection that we once gave ourselves to, letting it rule over us, now "no longer has mastery over us." We are truly free and, with that freedom, we're free to open our lives to the gift of the Holy Spirit.

3. Be filled with the Holy Spirit.

In Acts 8:9-25, there's a story of Peter and John being sent to Samaria because the Samaritans had believed in Jesus and needed direction:

> "When the apostles in Jerusalem heard that Samaria had accepted the word of God, they sent Peter and John to Samaria. When they arrived, they prayed for the new believers there that they might receive the Holy Spirit because the Holy Spirit had not yet come on any of them; they had simply been baptized in the name of the Lord Jesus. Then Peter and John placed their hands on them, and they received the Holy Spirit" (Acts 8:14-17).

We read here that the Samaritans had been baptized in water but hadn't received the Holy Spirit. Fixing this was simple: Peter and John prayed with them, and they were filled with the Holy Spirit. Once you believe in Jesus and allow His words to flow back into your heart, your spirit is born again. It comes back to life.

You then have a spirit that you don't know and have never used before. You must then learn how to exercise your own spirit to grow in the Holy Spirit. The first step to this is to receive the gift of the Holy Spirit Jesus promised you. As you pray to receive the Holy Spirit, God is faithful to fill you with the Holy Spirit and provide His power, His presence, and His help to grow in the Spirit.

In Acts 2:4, after obeying Jesus' command to wait for the Holy Spirit, we read that "all of them were filled with the Holy Spirit and began to speak in other tongues as the

Spirit enabled them." Paul describes praying in tongues or praying in the Holy Spirit by saying, "In the same way, the Spirit helps us in our weakness. We do not know what we ought to pray for, but the Spirit himself intercedes for us through wordless groans" (Romans 8:26).

4. Live out the first four of the *Forgotten Pieces* to grow your in life in the Spirit.

The Bible tells us that God is Spirit, so life in the Holy Spirit is really about learning how to interact with God. Hearing and responding to God's voice are good ways to begin. Growing in your ability to live each moment in connection with God, being aware of, and paying attention to His presence are other important ways. Living according to what God says to you, even when it is uncomfortable, is another way to grow in the Holy Spirit. Stepping into God's purposes for your life will deepen your life in the Holy Spirit.

We exist in three parts: We have physical bodies that contain our five senses (sight, hearing, taste, smell, and touch), and we also have souls. Souls contain all of the things about us that we can't touch physically but are nevertheless parts of our lives—our personalities, wills, intellectual capacities, feelings or emotions, consciences, and preferences. Finally, we have our spirits, now born again. Life in the Spirit involves all of the three parts of us including body, soul, and spirit.

God directs you through your spirit by His Holy Spirit, telling your mind and will what He wants for you; then you choose to obey and your body acts on what He has told you to do. The more practice you get in the first four things, the more fluidly you begin to live in the Holy Spirit and the stronger your life in the Holy Spirit becomes.

At first, just trying to hear His voice is a huge step and requires big faith. As you grow stronger and go deeper, you achieve moments when, although circumstances are going in one direction, you hear God speak to you, telling you to do something that would seem impossible in the natural. You step out in obedience to His direction and see miracles happen, just as Jesus said you would. This is the power of life in the Holy Spirit.

5. Learn to yield to the Holy Spirit.

God told Adam in the Garden, "You are free to eat from any tree in the garden; but you must not eat from the tree of the knowledge of good and evil, for when you eat from it you will certainly die" (Genesis 2:16-17). When Adam and Eve disobeyed and disconnected from God by eating the fruit from that tree, God's words proved to be true. Believing in Jesus allows our spirits to be born again, and baptism in water and then baptism in the Holy Spirit transfers our lives into His Kingdom, filling us with His life and power. Still, our bodies have within them the residue of the spiritual death we experienced, which we call "sin."

With each step toward God, each moment of listening to and responding to His voice and direction grows the life of the Spirit in you, and thus sin's power in your life is weakened. Yet the opposite is also true. Each time you pull back from believing and away from God's voice, you listen to the enemy's words, and sin grows stronger in you and consequently your spiritual strength is diminished.

As you continually interact with God and receive His grace and His power through the Holy Spirit, your brokenness is repaired and takes a backseat in your life. This is a fight you will engage in until the day you die but it's not a fair fight, for John tells us, "The one who is in you is greater than the one who is in the world" (1 John 4:4). It is wise to think of yourself as a spiritual athlete, constantly training to keep yourself growing in life in the Holy Spirit and, as a result, weakening sin's hold on you.

6. Follow the Holy Spirit into changing lives.

We have no record of any miracles Jesus performed prior to being filled with the Holy Spirit. Once He was "filled with the Holy Spirit" and "led by the Holy Spirit," He launched into three years of demonstrating God's love and power, changing people's lives practically while opening their hearts to His Father's love for them. As He neared the end of these three years, He made it clear to His disciples that He would ask the Father and that they would be given the gift of the Holy Spirit (see John 14:12). Jesus' life and ministry, so electrifying with miraculous power, are offered to us as a model for how we can live and impact others as

He did. Therefore, Jesus is our teacher and invites us to become His disciples as He guides us into learning to lean on the power of the Holy Spirit to reach the hearts of those He places around us.

Before He impacted those around Him in the Spirit, Jesus received all He needed from the Holy Spirit. Jesus' ministry to people came first out of the ministry He had received. He knew how the Spirit would care for and help others, because the Spirit helped Him. He knew how the Spirit would enable others to perform miracles, because it was this way for Him.

So it is with our lives, we receive ministry from the Trinity through the work of the Holy Spirit and are led to help others into the same experience. As we participate in ministry with Him, God also ministers to us, and our ability to be faithfully led into the work of the Spirit expands.

You'll be different when you live your life in the power of the Holy Spirit. He is so creative, so counterintuitive, so gifted, that when you live by His leading, your life will be totally changed. The reason you should learn to live this way is because every act of faith and every meaningful heart change is made possible because of the Holy Spirit. You need His Spirit to hear and obey Him. You need the Spirit to live in intimacy with Him, to live a life of faith even when there's pain. And you'll need the Holy Spirit in order to find and live out God's purpose for your life. The Spirit makes the other four pieces possible. The Spirit makes all things possible. And you'll need to learn to live in His power.

CHAPTER 25

LIVING LIFE IN THE POWER OF THE HOLY SPIRIT: A SUMMARY

To live your life in the power of the Holy Spirit is to live creatively, amazingly, and differently than anything you have ever seen in the whole world. The Holy Spirit is God's Spirit alive in your once-dead heart, now giving you direction and help.

Each of the other four **forgotten pieces** are infinitely more possible when you live your life in the power of the Holy Spirit, and a Spirit-filled life makes the other four more possible. In order to be led by the Spirit, you'll have to submit to Him, giving up any place where you're led by your own ideas, emotions, or sin. You'll need to be open to His deep creativity and sensitive to His ever-present voice. When you live in the power of the Holy Spirit, you'll live a life unlike any that is possible on your own.

In this section, we explored this life-changing **forgotten piece**, and we shared reasons why and how to learn to live your life in the power of the Holy Spirit.

Why live your life in the power of the Holy Spirit?

1. You were made for life in the Spirit.

2. You get what Jesus promised you.

3. You get continuous access to the One who is greater than anything in the world.

4. You become like Jesus.

5. You receive comfort from God, the only comfort that satisfied your heart.

6. You gain access to the fruit and gifts of the Holy Spirit.

7. You are healed and filled, and then, you overflow.

How do you live your life in the power of the Holy Spirit?

1. Take up your cross, deny yourself, and follow Him.

2. Be water baptized.

3. Be filled with the Spirit.

4. Live out the first four **Forgotten Pieces** to grow in life in the Spirit.

5. Learn to yield to the Holy Spirit.

6. Follow the Holy Spirit into changing lives.

This **forgotten piece** was left behind because the Holy Spirit will challenge every thing that's natural in you. It will contradict your sinful patterns and cause you step out into a faith that isn't understandable to the world. When this **forgotten piece** is remembered, you join Him on an epic adventure and you get in on an amazing part of a life of faith. The Holy Spirit is God working on Earth by living in human hearts. He makes all works of faith possible. He is miraculous. He is our helper. He is our guide. And living a life in the power of the Holy Spirit will lead to miraculous, amazing, necessary, and beautiful stories that can and will change the whole world.

A SUMMARY OF THE FIVE FORGOTTEN PIECES

The five **Forgotten Pieces** are essential tools for your faith journey. They aren't words on a page for you to passively read and then ignore. You'll need to step out in faith and live them out, and learn and grow with them. These tools have changed the lives of thousands of young people and leaders across the world. If you make them part of your life, they'll change everything for you, too.

The five **Forgotten Pieces** are:

1. **Learning to Hear and Obey God's Voice:** "Man does not live by bread alone but by every word that comes from the mouth of God" (Matthew 4:4).

> God speaks, and you'll need to learn to hear Him and obey Him in order to receive the direction and help you need for your life.

2. **Learning to Live in Moment-to-Moment Intimacy with God:** "Apart from Me you can do nothing" (John 15:5) .

> You'll need to learn to seek and to live in His presence, abiding in the Vine. It is key to growing

your relationships with Jesus in His power and love.

3. **Embracing a Life of Faith and Pain:** «[Jesus] learned obedience through what He suffered" (Hebrews 5:8).

> Suffering is a tool God uses to develop hope in you as you learn to wait on the Lord to fulfill His Word and promises to you in the midst of conflicting circumstances. If this is true of Him, it will be true for you. When you learn to transcend pain instead of avoiding it, you can accomplish things in the Lord that would be impossible otherwise.

4. **Finding and Fulfilling God's Purpose for Your Life:** "Without a vision the people perish" (Proverbs 29:18).

> Adam. Noah. Abraham. Joseph. Moses. Samuel. David. Jesus. Few leaders in the Bible went very far without God revealing pieces of His purpose for their lives. You'll do better at facing the ups and downs of God's process of development when you can see that it is headed somewhere wonderful.

5. **Learning to Live in the Power of the Holy Spirit:** "'Not by might, nor by power but by My Spirit,' says the Lord" (Zechariah 4:6).

> Today many people act spiritual but are missing His power and fruitfulness in their lives. You'll need to learn to walk by faith into yielding to the power and direction of the Holy Spirit. When you do, you'll turn the world upside down.

These **forgotten pieces** must be recovered, and remembered. They were tools Jesus used to obey God, live in constant connection with Him, and change the entire world. They will need to make a strong return into your life and the lives of those who follow Jesus.

CONCLUSION

There's a stark contrast between the way humans have historically tried to share or pass on their faith and the way that God does it. We write books that detail the things we are convinced people need to believe. God breaks into people's lives and hews out a friendship using the chisel and hammer of time and experiences. Humans create systematic programs about relating to God that are taught in classrooms, while God invites people into sweat-stained, sun-soaked adventures, led by His presence and voice. We punctuate our approach with quizzes and final exams while God does so with miracles, setting people free from dark traps while giving and fulfilling promises.

The **forgotten pieces** described in these previous chapters cannot simply be handed to you. However, the words in this book may be used by God to invite you into your own unique, friendship-forming journey with Him. This book puts in print the intentions of God's own heart to do whatever it takes to help you begin to recognize and respond to His presence and voice. This book can inspire you through how God has helped other leaders across history follow His direction into impossible and uncomfortable situations as they endured the pain of waiting for His hand to move and then experienced the power of His salvation and deliverance. The clear intimation is that what He did for them, He's just as ready to do it for you. You too can be set free from shallow ideas and invisible shackles that have kept you running in circles for too many years.

This book makes some promises that can be summarized in a single statement: You were designed to live in a life-defining relationship with the God who created you and that same God has even given you access to every resource you need to become His friend. Oh, that you will tune your ears and heart to hear the seemingly outlandish promises that this promise-making, promise-keeping God so loves to make. Oh, that you will then walk into the highest, deepest levels of friendship possible with God as you see Him make these promises come true before your eyes—often after the most circuitous and unintelligible routes you could have ever imagined.

You won't "graduate" from any of these five things. They won't become old tools buried deep within your intellectual attic. Like walking, breathing, eating, and drinking, they will become a part of you, a part of your journey. Every day, every month, every year will bring breakthroughs, innovations, and new understanding about each one. Just as often, you'll find that these **forgotten pieces** push you deeper and deeper into loving, searching, and responding in obedience to Scripture. They will make the Bible come alive, and they will make you hunger to read more, know more, and live out more.

These things will also change your relationship with the body of Christ expressed in a local congregation. Whatever "church" or "churches" have been for you up to this point, these five **forgotten pieces** will lead you to lay down your life for the people in those churches because you will experience "home" and love in their midst in ways that are new and change everything. Church will never again be a building to you. Your church will be a gloriously imperfect spiritual family that requires the best of you in what will be a lifelong wrestling match.

You will need to show grace, love, support and what seem to be bottomless fountains of patience. At the same time, you will need to raise your voice to challenge and confront these very same family members when God says to do so. This wrestling isn't for the faint of heart but God is in it. He invites us to wrestle with Him and pushes us to wrestle with one another, providing each other with the mutual accountability necessary to grow in the kind of faith that Samuel, John, Paul, Abraham, and Peter had.

There's something wonderful and unexpected about

building these core and eternal aspects of your relationship with God. Each of these five pieces of building your relationship with Him carries with them an exponential power. After years of listening to God's voice and being directed by Him, your life will be built on His Word, His wisdom, and His will. With each day, you will be directed more and more by His omniscience, His omnipotence, and His love. Like Samuel, John, Paul, Abraham, and Peter, His voice, His presence, a life of hope in Him, of pursuing His purpose, and living in the power of His Spirit will unleash faith and His presence into your life, leading you into things that you don't yet have the capacity to grasp.

As was mentioned in the beginning of this book, Boy With a Ball's work with young leaders in the U.S., Latin America, and Africa over the past twenty years has made it clear that it's impossible to grow in these five things without the three tools of a coach, a team, and a playing field. Because these things each involve invisible, spiritual growth in areas that are contrary to the ways and cultures of this world, in the beginning growing in them will feel very much like trying to fly or to breathe underwater. Each of these **forgotten pieces** are completely possible but they involve growing in the kind of faith that led Peter to take steps onto the surface of a lake. It's easy to talk yourself out of these things, easy to give up on them, and easy to take a few steps into them, settling for superficial experiences in each. Don't choose a lesser version. Use the tools and press onward.

If these **forgotten pieces** remain forgotten in your life, your faith and relationship with God will wither away, overcome by the wind and waves of a world around you. You'll start to give way to believing there's little or no use for an invisible God whose ways are so different from yours. After a while, not growing in your relationship with Jesus in these ways will end in you walking away from your faith or, maybe worse, sticking around as your relationship with God degrades into dry religion. We live in a world that is rejecting Christianity because of a version of it that has forgotten these important facets of knowing, trusting, and loving Jesus. They're most often not truly rejecting Jesus but rejecting our shallow, dry versions of what it means to "know" Him without really knowing Him.

However, If we get these things, everything changes. On the most personal level, the same resurrection power and life that was displayed so potently in Jesus will flow through your heart and relationships. Your own heart will thrive:

> "But blessed is the one who trusts in the Lord, whose confidence is in him. He is like a tree planted by the waters that sends out its roots toward the stream. It does not fear when the heat comes, and its leaves are always green. It does not worry in a year of drought, nor does it cease to produce fruit" (Jeremiah 17:7-8).

And these things will go out beyond ourselves to produce supernatural, exceptional life change for those around us. These **forgotten pieces** at work within and through us can only change everything. In our world that is lost, that is dry, that is aching, these things are counter-cultural streams of life, hope, and promise.

As exciting as *The Forgotten Pieces* are to read about, they are exceptional to live out.

Now, go.

ENDNOTES

PREFACE

[1] King Jr., Dr. Martin Luther. "Rediscovering Lost Values." *The Martin Luther King Jr. Research and Education Institute.* Address, February 28, 1954. https://kinginstitute.stanford.edu/king-papers/documents/rediscovering-lost-values-0.

INTRODUCTION: THREE TOOLS YOU WILL NEED

[2] *The Matrix.* United States: Warner Bros, 1999.

[3] Lewis, C.S. *The Lion, the Witch, and the Wardrobe.* Geoffrey Bles, 1950.

CHAPTER 6: THE APOSTLE JOHN: THE ONE JESUS LOVED

[4] Tozer, A.W. *The Divine Conquest.* Christian Publications, 1950.

CHAPTER 8: HOW TO LIVE IN MOMENT-TO-MOMENT INTIMACY WITH GOD?

[5] Brother Lawrence. *The Practice of the Presence of God.* Whitaker House, 1982.

CHAPTER 13: WHY EMBRACE A LIFE OF FAITH AND PAIN?

[6] Kierekegaard, Soren. *Fear and Trembling.* Penguin Classics, 1986.

[7] Lewis, C.S. *The Chronicles of Narnia Series.* HarperCollins, 1950.

[8] "Chréstotés." Strong's Greek: 5544. χρηστότης (chréstotés) -- goodness, excellence, uprightness, 2001. https://biblehub.com/greek/5544.htm.

CHAPTER 11: WHY FIND AND FULFILL GOD'S PURPOSE FOR YOUR LIFE?

[9] *Rocky.* United States: United Artists, 1976.

ABOUT THE AUTHORS

Jamie Johnson

Jamie Johnson's life changed when Jesus walked into his high school Algebra class. Coming out of his own hurt and pain, Jamie was so impacted by the way the Lord healed and helped him, he immediately turned outward to see it happen again for those around him. Jamie began his career as a youth developer when he was sixteen in a small church's youth group in Florida. In college, the Lord gave him a vision: what if you could create teams like leagues of superheroes that go out to impact their cities? From this, Boy With a Ball was born.

What began as one team in San Antonio, Texas has grown into an international organization with teams across Africa, Latin America, the Middle East, and the U.S.A. Jamie currently serves as the Executive Director for Boy With a Ball. He and his wife, Kathy, have three adult children and live in Atlanta, Georgia. Jamie and Kathy have given their lives to help young people reach their God-given purpose.

Originally from Tennessee, Molly Johnson grew up in North Georgia. When she met Jesus in eighth grade, her heart filled with this hope that our God is a God who speaks to us. Molly joined Boy With a Ball as an intern in college and began to grow as she learned that He is in fact a God who speaks specifically and constantly to her heart. Through campus ministries and Boy With a Ball's work, Molly experienced the Lord's breakthrough for those around her, and she uncovered part of her purpose to give her life for helping young people. Molly is currently the Communications Director for Boy with a Ball. She, her husband, Joey, and her son live in Atlanta, Georgia.

Molly Johnson

BOY WITH A BALL

Boy With a Ball is an international non-profit that reaches and equips young people to turn and transform their communities. We are a growing movement of leaders, donors, volunteers, churches, schools, and businesses that have turned outward to impact the cities we live in.

For more than twenty years, we have launched growing leaders into the five Forgotten Pieces. We have seen many come to know Him and find His purpose. And we have seen entire communities transformed because of God's ever-present work in neighborhoods around the world.

Follow us on Facebook, Instagram, and LinkedIn.

〇　　　f　　　in

@boywithaball

FOR MORE BOY WITH A BALL RESOURCES, VISIT

FORGOTTENPIECES.COM

boywithaball.com | info@boywithaball.com
PO BOX 748, Buford, GA 30515